IN CONCERT SING

IN CONCERT SING

Concerning hymns and their usage

by

Bertram L. Barnby

Foreword by

John Habgood

The Canterbury Press
Norwich

First published 1996 by The Canterbury Press Norwich
(a publishing imprint of Hymns Ancient & Modern Limited,
a registered charity)
St Mary's Works, St Mary's Plain,
Norwich, Norfolk, NR3 3BH

British Library Cataloguing in Publication Data

A catalogue record for this book is available
from the British Library

ISBN 1-85311-153-8

Typeset by David Gregson Associates
Beccles, Suffolk and
Printed and bound in Great Britain by
Athenæum Press Ltd, Gateshead, Tyne & Wear

TO
HARRY CURREN

Let Saints on earth in concert sing

—*Charles Wesley (1707–88)*

FOREWORD

THIS IS A BOOK to delight any hymn-lover, to convert those who have never really thought much about hymns, and to guide those with the responsibility of choosing them for worship. It radiates a love and understanding of hymnody which should be infectious, and it is full of good advice.

In an age when much traditional hymn-singing is being replaced by trivial and repetitive choruses, this reminder of a rich resource is all the more important. Furthermore, as the author tellingly reminds us, it is an ecumenical resource. Hymns can unite even where liturgies divide. And it is not only in corporate worship that hymns are significant. Many people's personal spirituality is rooted in the words of hymns, remembered from Sunday school or school assembly, and these may well provide the only words available to such people for prayer.

Canon Barnby is to be congratulated on this highly readable and scholarly introduction to an important subject. I can warmly commend it.

JOHN HABGOOD

CONTENTS

AUTHOR'S PREFACE

THIS BOOK IS ABOUT HYMNS, their meaning, their music and their use. It is offered not only to clergy and musicians, but also to the increasing number of laymen and laywomen who serve on worship committees of all denominations, as well as to the millions of regular viewers of *Songs of Praise* on television and listeners to hymn-singing on the radio. It is written as a humble contribution to the Decade of Evangelism in the belief that the hymns we sing together are our sincerest expressions of worship and bring people of all denominations and none closer to the unity for which Christ prayed.

Christians have been singing hymns for close on 2000 years. The number of hymns in the English language alone runs into hundreds of thousands. The field is immense. As a rule, therefore, I have made no more than passing reference to hymns peculiar to one denomination. Most of the hymns discussed are the common heritage of all Christians in Britain, America and throughout the English-singing world. Indeed I go so far as to claim that, next to the Bible, nothing unites us more than hymn-singing.

The approach of this book is wide: theological, musical, literary and liturgical. It is my conviction that only when considered from all these points of view can a hymn be fairly judged and effectively used.

In part 1 we shall see that from earliest times the Church has sung to God in praise and prayer, and to its members about its faith and way of life. Thus all aspects of public worship—praise, prayer, teaching and exhortation—have found expression in hymns. To correct what I believe to be the mistaken notion that all hymns are addressed to God, I have devoted chapters 3 to 6 to discussing well-known hymns under those four headings. Chapter 2, an interlude, is an attempt to answer the question. 'What makes a good hymn?'

Part 2 stresses the importance of music. Since a hymn does not live until it is sung, no study of hymnody is complete that does not take its music into consideration. In chapters 7 and

8 guidelines are given for judging a tune: in chapter 7 as music and in chapter 8 as the right vehicle for the words. The right tune can give a hymn immortality, the wrong tune can smother it at birth. In chapter 9 our rich and varied heritage of hymn-tunes is displayed.

Part 3 concerns the art of choosing hymns for public worship. Some basic principles are laid down and then applied to the regular liturgical services of the Church of England. Nonconformists, for historical reasons, have long been hymn-conscious and have developed an instinct for using hymns as companions to worship. As an Anglican, I am conscious of my own Church's need to take this art more seriously. I hope my Free-Church friends will take this as a compliment and find these pages of interest, if only to see how much I have learnt from them. I hope too that Roman Catholics—who treasure their liturgical tradition like us—and have an even shorter experience of modern hymnody—will be encouraged to value the use of hymns to illuminate and enrich their services.

Of the making of hymn books there is no end. In the present century alone, the hymnals of each of the main Christian denominations have been revised several times (not to mention the addition of supplements), each edition having a different set of hymn numbers. This presents a problem in providing references. As most of the hymns discussed in part 1 are well known and common to all Churches, I have generally not given references, since to do so would mean the cumbersome insertion of ten or more to each hymn. Readers who wish to look up a hymn in their own hymn book will find help in David Perry's *Hymns and Tunes Indexed* (Hymn Society and RSCM, 1980).

In part 2 I have assumed that hymn-tune enthusiasts will possess at least a copy of the *New English Hymnal* of 1986 and *Hymns Ancient & Modern* of 1983. Most of the best tunes will be found in one or the other.

Since for the purpose of study, it is desirable to have before one, if possible, the hymns as the authors wrote them, I refer the reader to the preface to the first edition of the *English Hymnal* (reprinted in 1933), which states that the editor made a principle of this. For the same reason I have chosen to refer to the *Anglican Hymn Book*, as representative of the Evangelical party, rather than the more up-to-date *Hymns for Today's Church*, in which many hymns have been altered almost beyond recognition.

For the convenience of general readers I have avoided as much as possible the use of musical, literary and theological terms. Where they occur they are explained in passing or in the glossary at the end of the book. Letters of the Greek alphabet are replaced by their English equivalents. Some musical quotations are included for the interest of musicians (plainsong in modern notation), but to indicate individual notes and short phrases the sol-fa names are used. This saves space and avoids confusion as to key. Occasionally I have suggested a tune or arrangement not hitherto published as particularly suited to certain words. Should there be sufficient demand I will try to make these available.

Like all writers on this subject I am indebted to Julian's *Dictionary of Hymnology* and to the historical editions of *Hymns Ancient & Modern* (1909 and 1962) for valuable background information. I also record my thanks to the Chetham Library, Manchester, for permission to reproduce their facsimile of John Byrom's manuscript of 'Christians, awake!', which they possess; and to the Syndics of the Fitzwilliam Museum, Cambridge, who gave me a photograph of their original manuscript of Handel's three hymn-tunes with permission to include it in this book.

Writing on hymns today is like trying to board a moving train. While I was engaged in this work, others were writing on the same subject, notably: Lionel Dakers, *Choosing and Using Hymns* (1986); Ian Bradley, *The Penguin Book of Hymns* (1990); Charles Robertson, *Singing the Faith: a symposium* (1990); Baker and Welsby, *Hymns and Hymn-singing* (1993); Donald Davie, *The 18th-Century Hymn in England* (1993); and Brian Castle, *Sing a New Song to the Lord* (1994). On examining them, I find that for the most part they cover different ground. Where we have crossed paths I hope I have acknowledged them. If inadvertently I have failed to do so, I beg the authors' pardon and their publishers'.

It remains for me to thank those who have helped me. Harry Curren read each chapter as it was written, spotted errors, made valuable suggestions, and compiled the Glossary and Index. Richard Southey and Joan Mannings typed the whole book on their home computers. In writing on the crisis in authority, I found it a help to discuss it with my friend Stuart Westley who, as a teacher, had inside experience of it. For information on the singing of 'Abide with me' at the Cup Final I am obliged to the Football Association and to Peter Swales. When the book was nearing completion, my friend and former colleague Bishop John Gaisford mentioned it to the then Archbishop of York, who found time in his busy life to read the typescript and write a foreword. To all of these, and to my wife, whose patience and co-operation made the work possible, I am profoundly grateful. On going to press I wish to express my thanks to the editorial staff of The Canterbury Press Norwich for their valued help and advice.

August 1996 B.L. BARNBY

ABBREVIATIONS

AH	Anglican Hymn Book
A&M	Hymns Ancient & Modern (1983, unless otherwise stated)
AMR	Hymns Ancient & Modern Revised (1950)
ASB	Alternative Service Book
AV	Authorised Version of the Bible
BBC	British Broadcasting Corporation
BCP	Book of Common Prayer
CCH	Complete Celebration Hymnal (RC)
CMS	Church Missionary Society
EH	English Hymnal (1906)
H&P	Hymns and Psalms (Methodist)
HTC	Hymns for Today's Church
MP	Mission Praise
NEB	New English Bible
NEH	New English Hymnal (1986)
NT	New Testament
OBC	Oxford Book of Carols
OT	Old Testament
RC	Roman Catholic
RSCM	Royal School of Church Music
RSV	Revised Standard Version of the Bible
St	Saint
SP	Songs of Praise
SPCK	Society for Promotion of Christian Knowledge
SPG	Society for the Propagation of the Gospel (now USPG)
URC	United Reformed Church
WS	Worship Songs A&M
WOV	With One Voice
WH	Westminster Hymnal

together. The publication of *The Baptist Church Hymnal* in 1900 supports this claim.

Mention should here be made of the American revivalists, Dwight Moody and Ira Sankey, who visited this country in 1872 and 1882. Their hymn-book *Sacred Songs and Solos* featured a new style of hymn. These unpretentious lyrics, with tunes to match, served their purpose well. At least a dozen of them, still to be heard today, have lost nothing of their relevance or appeal.

Meanwhile A&M was continuing its triumphant career: an 1868 appendix and an 1875 revised edition brought its total of hymns to 473, and an 1889 supplement to 638. By then it had become, as Erik Routley put it, a national institution. On the whole the literary standards of Heber and Montgomery were not maintained. Selection committees seem to have cared more for popular taste than literary quality. By the Nineties, however, the Education Act of 1870 was beginning to take effect: the rising generation was better equipped to appreciate good poetry and music. Julian's Dictionary (1892) had aroused interest in hymnology. The time was ripe for appraisal.

Already in 1884 the Free-Churchman William Garrett Horder had published *Congregational Hymns*, restricting his selection, as he says in his preface, 'to such hymns as join the fervour of religious emotion, the ring of poetic expression, with the chastened sobriety of scriptural truth'. Many fine hymns, some from America, first introduced to English worshippers by Garrett Horder have since become favourites.

Another pioneer of hymnic reform was the poet Robert Bridges. Having embarked on a medical career, he wrote poetry in his spare time. In his late thirties, however, he gave up his practice, settled at Yattendon in Berkshire, and devoted himself to literature. Eventually he became Poet Laureate. Being a devout Anglican and an able musician, he took an interest in his parish-church choir, of which for nine years he was precentor. His *Yattendon Hymnal* (1899) had been issued in instalments as a supplement to the book already in use—probably A&M. Its prime purpose was to restore old tunes to their original form and rhythm. This called for new words to fit them. The hymns Bridges wrote for this purpose are examples of that 'ring of poetic expression' Garrett Horder had looked for; they are also models of how music and words should be matched. See, for instance, 'Happy are they, they that love God' and 'The duteous day now closeth'.

Meanwhile a radical revision of A&M was in preparation. After nine years of unspeakable toil, countless meetings of the committee and sub-committees, consultations, questionnaires and doubtless much prayer, the book appeared in 1904. It was a failure.

With hindsight we can see that the rock on which the new edition foundered was the success of its predecessors. To create a national institution and then alter it is fatal. The hymns popularised by A&M, with their faults as well as their merits, had taken root in folk memory. Any change, even for the better, was regarded as sacrilege. The very numbers were holy: the fact that 'Abide with me' was no longer 27 caused an outcry. Another factor was the drastic revision of the music, which we shall consider in Chapter 9.

All was not lost, however. The *Historical Edition* (1908) by W.H. Frere, a prominent member of the committee and later Bishop of Truro, is a monument to the scholarship and dedication involved in the preparation of the ill-fated edition. It is a standard work second only to Julian. Neither was A&M dead. The old edition with the supplement of 1889 continued to sell. A second supplement, under the musical editorship of Sir Sydney Nicholson, was added in 1916, and in 1922 the old—unaltered but for the addition of alternative tunes—and the two supplements were bound in one volume called the *Standard Edition*. This typical English compromise was successful: in this form A&M held its place until the revision of 1950.

The spate of hymns abated at the close of the Victorian era. A time of consolidation followed: existing hymnals were revised—notably *Church Hymns* (SPCK, 1903)—and some new ones appeared.

If A&M was the epoch-making hymnbook of the nineteenth century, that of the twentieth was surely the *English*

Hymnal (1906), EH for short, produced by Percy Dearmer and a small group of like minded men of vision and taste. Ralph Vaughan Williams, then a promising young musician, was chosen as musical editor because he had declared: 'But I know nothing about hymns.' This epitomises the attitude of Dearmer and his friends. They wanted a fresh approach. Their aims are stated in the preface: 'The *English Hymnal* is a collection of the best hymns in the English language and is offered as a humble companion to the Book of Common Prayer.' The operative word is 'best'. They were not interested in perpetuating second rate hymns and tunes simply because they were popular. In any case many such, as well as some of the first rank, were excluded by copyright. With an eye to Garrett Horder, Dearmer cast his net wide, selecting what he considered artistically good and theologically sound from all ages and denominations.

For instance, he did not reject 'City of God, how broad and far' because its author, the American Samuel Johnson, had Unitarian sympathies. This and other fine American hymns appeared for the first time in an Anglican hymnal. Likewise works by great English poets, notably George Herbert, Christina Rossetti and Robert Bridges, were included. The social gospel, nearly twenty years before our first Labour government, finds hymnic expression in 'When wilt thou save the people' by the Sheffield poet, Ebenezer Elliot, as also in G.K. Chesteron's 'O God of earth and altar', Henry Scott-Holland's 'Judge eternal, throned in splendour' and 'Once to every man and nation'—Horder's skilful adaptation of lines from Russell Lowell's American poem 'The Present Crisis' (1845). As a general rule hymns, even translations, are given in the book as their authors wrote them. The same applies to the music, as we shall see in Chapter 9. The resultant variety of styles brought a breath of fresh air into Anglican worship. The very binding of EH is symbolic: bright green, the colour of growth.

Though 'not a party book', according to its preface, EH was welcomed by Anglo-Catholics for its ample provision of eucharistic and office hymns. It also found its way into cathedrals, college chapels, and parish churches aspiring to a lofty standard of worship. It is a tribute to its forward-thinking editor that EH, its text unaltered, held its place in a growing number of churches until the New EH was published in 1986—after eighty years in which the Church, and indeed the world, changed almost beyond recognition.

Dearmer was an artist and a humanitarian, who believed in the Church of England and in his vision of what its worship and mission might be. This vision was broadened by his experiences in the First World War, notably as chaplain to the Red Cross. In 1925 he edited *Songs of Praise* (SP): it contained 470 hymns, with a core from EH. On the day of publication it was adopted by Liverpool Cathedral; it soon became popular with liberal Evangelicals. Its wide use in schools fostered good taste in hymns among the rising generation. As the first attempt at an undenominational hymnal, SP paved the way for *The BBC Hymnbook* (1951) and *With One Voice* (first published in Australia 1977). In preparing the Enlarged Edition of 1931, Dearmer was prevailed upon to depart from his former principle and alter texts to suit all schools of thought. This regrettable step laid the book open to the charge of vague theism. Otherwise its literary standard justifies the Editor's claim: 'In the future, intelligent men will be able to take up a hymn book and read it with as much interest and appreciation as any other collection of poetry and music.'

Dearmer died in 1936. Three years later the Second World War interrupted the work of reappraisal he had initiated. In the early Fifties appeared three important hymnals on which work had begun before the war: *A&M Revised* in 1950 and, the following year, *The BBC Hymn Book* and *Congregational Praise.* Even the *Baptist Hymnal* (third edition, 1962), *Hymns for Church and School* (1964) and the *Anglican Hymn Book* (1965) show little sign of the hymn explosion that was to follow.

Social changes from 1945 onwards awakened the Church to such issues as human rights, race relations, church unity and world peace. By the early Sixties, hymn-writers were turning their attention to these topics. Moreover, congregations of all denominations began to see themselves as a family rather than a gathering of individuals—and that family centred on the Eucharist. A forward movement was afoot.

At about this time, however, the wind of change began to blow up some clouds which had been gathering since the end of the war. The rising generation, having seen the disastrous consequences of obedience to the unbridled authority of tyrants like Hitler, became suspicious of all authority: parents, teachers, government, the Church, even God. Traditional standards were overturned. Discipline, respect, obedience and taste came to be regarded as dirty words. Many state schools, ostensibly in deference to ethnic minorities, dropped assembly and ceased to give specifically Christian teaching. Preachers neglected the transcendence of God in favour of his immanence; they stressed the manhood rather than the divinity of Christ, duty to neighbour rather than duty to God. Even the 'new orthodoxy' of C. S. Lewis and Dorothy Sayers, which had steadied the Church of the Forties and Fifties, was scorned in certain quarters.

All this unsettled Church and society alike. A generation has since grown up without God, and hence without a refuge in trouble; without standards, and hence turning to violence and crime; without hope, and hence despairing. The miracle is that so many young people still found the faith. To me it is significant that close on the heels of the crisis in authority came the Charismatic revival, founded on the words of St Peter in Acts 2:39, from which we may infer that the gifts of the Spirit at Pentecost are still available to those with sufficient faith. Its emphasis on faith, prayer, caring, healing and not least, hymn—singing has—despite the more bizarre features of the movement caught the imagination of young and old and brought life and a sense of direction to churches of all traditions.

The changes and trends of these turbulent times are reflected by the many hymn-writers of the last thirty years. Space would fail me to discuss them here. In any case we shall be meeting many of them in later chapters. Meanwhile, to save the reader's time, I have selected a dozen or so modern writers and tabulated their hymn-book appearances. A figure after a plus denotes translations.

Authors Born	A&M 1982	*Worship Songs A&M* 1992	*New English Hymnal* 1986	*Hymns for Today's Church* 1982	U.R.C. *Rejoice and Sing* 1991	*Baptist Praise and Worship* 1991	R.C. *Celeb'n Hymnal* 1984	*Methodist Hymns and Psalms* 1983	*Broadcast Praise* 1981	*Mission Praise* 1983	*With One Voice* 1979
F Pratt Green 1903	12	5	1	4	11+1	9+1	3	27	6	1	3
Sydney Carter 1915	4	1	1		2	2	2	1			3
J Quinn 1919	3	1	2	1	5	1	11+1	1	1		8+1
B Foley 1919	3	1	2	2	2	4		4	1		2
T Dudley-Smith 1926	2	6	6	46	5	15	1	9	1	15	1
S Temple 1928		1			1		14			1	
F Kaan 1929	9	1		3	21+2	7	7+2	8	3		6+1
M Saward 1932		1		26		2				3	
B Wren 1936	8	2	1	6	12+1	6		9+1	4		1+1
C Idle 1938		6	1	35		8		1		4	
D Mowbray 1938				16		3		1			
M Perry 1942		4		41	1	8		1		1	
J Bell 1949 *and* G Maule 1958		7			7	2					
G Kendrick 1954		2			4	7				29	

It will be noted that the first half-dozen authors belong to an earlier generation which started writing hymns in later life. Sydney Carter was the only one to adopt an unchurchy style. The others were content to express new ideas in traditional verse forms. Fred Pratt Green, already known as preacher and poet, had retired from the Methodist ministry before he began to write hymns. Many of his are included in all the collections listed. The only other modern author to share this distinction is the Anglican bishop, Timothy Dudley-Smith, whose 'Tell out, my soul'—not written as a hymn—is now sung throughout the English-singing world. Less prolific but none the less important are the Roman Catholic contributors, Brian Foley, James Quinn and Sebastian Temple. Fred Kaan of the URC, a campaigner for social justice, has written valuable hymns on the subject—though I agree with Cyril Taylor (*Hymns for Today Discussed*) that he has gone too far in 'Sing we a song of high revolt'. Brian Wren, also of the URC, has something new to say on many subjects. Graham Kendrick—originally Baptist—wrote the words and music of his songs. On his style opinions differ, but he always delivers a scriptural message. So does John Bell, who writes lyrics in tandem with Graham Maule, set to music by himself. The other writers listed are evangelical Anglicans who between them have contributed over a hundred hymns to HTC.

The hymnals included in our table are representative of the latest publications in this country. A&M (New Standard Edition, 1983) needs no introduction. *Worship Songs A&M* is an admirable bridge between traditional and popular. The quality of its music is assured by the editorial team. In comparison the *New EH* (1986) is conservative. It is, however, a compliment to the forward-looking editor of the first edition (1906) that about four-fifths of the metrical hymns in the new book are retained from the old. Moreover, NEH is designed to meet liturgical needs, particularly hymns on the saints, sadly lacking in other books. Many of the new hymns are by committee members, notably George Timms. A number of clergy will also appreciate the provision of responsorial psalms.

HTC has some valuable new hymns, though, in my view, the compilers have been over zealous in modernising the classics. The Baptist and Methodist Churches and the URC have each produced new books maintaining the high standard one has come to expect of them. The Complete *Celebration Hymnal* (1984) is the most widely used Roman

Catholic hymn book today. Of Ecumenical collections, *Mission Praise* (1983) (more than doubled in size in 1987) is a mixed bag designed for mission. The loose-leaf format suggests that it is not intended for posterity. Its sales justify this policy.

Reading our table horizontally as well as vertically, one is struck by the ecumenical trend of the recent output. It is significant that the most recent collections—*Baptist Praise and Worship* and *Worship Songs A&M*—are also the most comprehensive. From this it seems that, in hymn singing at least, we are still moving closer together. So history repeats itself. The early Christian fathers refuted heresy with sound doctrine; the Reformers corrected abuses in the light of scripture; Wesley and the Evangelicals confronted hopelessness with the gospel; the Tractarians met ignorance with teaching; to-day's Church is challenging secularism and apathy. In each case the Christian message has been expedited by the singing of the faith.

2 A GOOD HYMN

HYMN-WRITING is an applied art. A hymn cannot be judged by poetic standards alone. The first question is 'Does it achieve its purpose?' A crude street map, pencilled in haste on the back of an envelope, is good if it guides a stranger to his destination. Such were most of the revival and temperance hymns of a century ago which, it was claimed, reduced the population of hell by a million. If the same can be said of their counterparts today, these too are justified. The value of such hymns cannot be denied. Two things, however, should be remembered. First, they were not written for posterity but to meet a passing need. Second, their appeal is directed mainly to people outside the Church. Each generation produced a crop, most of which have their day and cease to be.

The danger is that their instant appeal may lead to their continued use in schools and churches after their purpose is served. Such associations formed at an impressionable age can influence the taste of a lifetime, engendering either an uncritical preference for bad art or, worse, disdain for the faith so expressed. Those responsible for worship in school or church would be wise to ensure that good literature and good music are associated with our religion.

As a companion to public worship a hymn should inspire the mind, stretch the imagination and yet appeal at every level. The hymn-writer walks a tightrope. Perhaps this is one reason why so few of our great poets have written hymns. Tennyson frankly admitted: 'A good hymn is the most difficult thing in the world to write. In a good hymn you have to be both commonplace and poetical.' Yet in his old age, at the request of his nurse, he wrote 'Crossing the Bar'. There is nothing commonplace in this simple, poetic statement of faith. His son's opinion, 'That is the crown of your life's work', seems to have been shared by the poet, whose last wish was: 'Mind you put "Crossing the Bar" at the end of all editions of my poems.'

Just over a century earlier William Cowper, one of the foremost poets of his age, when collaborating with John

Newton in the production of *Olney Hymns*, agreed to the principle that 'Imagery and colouring of poetry, if admitted at all, should be admitted very sparingly and with good judgement.' Yet in his best hymns Cowper managed to be both simple and poetic.

With such examples in mind, let us try to draw this difficult line. The limitations of a hymn are basically those of all lyric verse: it is short, simple and singable. The purpose of a hymn, however, limits freedom in each respect.

Lyric verse is short in comparison with epic, dramatic and romantic verse. Yet many sacred lyrics, in their original form, are too long to be hymns. The length of a hymn is determined by its use as an act of worship. For most purposes some twenty or thirty lines will suffice, though longer hymns may be needed to cover certain liturgical actions such as processions and the eucharistic offertory. As it is customary to sing each verse to the same tune, a long hymn with short verses can grow wearisome. Therefore the longer the hymn, the longer each verse should be. It also helps if the lines are varied in length. On the whole, compactness gives power to a hymn: wordiness enfeebles it. Hymn-writers share with preachers the temptation to stray from the point. The reader of the ensuing chapters may be surprised at the number of famous hymns that have been improved by shortening.

Simplicity, too, is more often a virtue than a limitation. It is not a case of inhibiting the muse but of avoiding words, phrases or images which cloud rather than clarify the sense. The result of this discipline is often better poetry. Consider the depth of thought in George Herbert's 'Teach me, my God and King', which, although not written with any thought of its being sung by a congregation in worship, was recognised as a superb hymn many years later. Yet, out of the 118 words in the five verses we sing today, 105 are monosyllables. As for imagery, the very title is an image: 'The Elixir'. The key is in the first and last verses:

Teach me, my God and King,
  In all things thee to see,
And what I do in anything
  To do it as for thee.

This is the famous stone
That turneth all to gold ...

The images in the intervening verses take up in turn the motifs of the opening prayer. 'in all things thee to see' is symbolized by glass, which one may look 'on' or 'through' 'as for thee' is the tincture that gives lustre to the dullest chore; and 'who sweeps a room' a homely example of its use.

It is interesting that Herbert made at least two revisions of this poem. (All three versions are given in full, with perceptive comments, by Helen White in chapter 7 of her book *The Metaphysical Poets.*) In his final revision he inserted a new second verse:

Not rudely, as a beast,
To run into an action
But still to make thee prepossest
And give it his perfection.

This verse is an example of what is acceptable in a poem but not in a hymn. The metrical irregularity of its double rhyme conveys poetically the crude impulsiveness of animal instinct; but when it is sung it strikes a jarring note of impishness. Moreover, the verbal economy of the last two lines obscures the sense. John Wesley, who first spotted this lyric as a possible hymn, included it in his earliest collection (1738); but much altered, and with an entirely new second verse. Modern editors wisely omit verse 2 altogether and print the rest as Herbert left it.

To be singable, by a body of people, a hymn needs rhythm. The rhythm of verse is its metre. Here perhaps some elementary remarks on prosody, the art of metre, may be helpful. The row of figures printed above the tune in most hymnbooks denotes the number of syllables in each line. The commonest forms, common metre (8 6 8 6), long metre (8 8 8 8) and short metre (6 6 8 6) are signified by their initials: CM, LM, SM. Eight-line verses in these metres as said to be in double common metre (DCM), and so on.

As a means of determining metre, however, syllable-counting falls short. Take two well-known hymns, 'We love the place, O God' and 'Lord', thy word abideth'. Both are designated 6 6 6 6, yet the ear will already have spotted a fundamental difference. In either case the line may be divided rhythmically into groups of two syllables but, whereas in the former the stress falls on the second syllable of each pair, in the latter it is on the first:

We lóve | the pláce | O Gód |
Lórd thy | wórd a- | bídeth |

These divisions of the line are called feet. The usual foot-patterns each have their names.

The Iamb is short–long and the Trochee is long–short, as in those examples. The anapaest is short–short–long:

When a Knight | won his spúrs | in the stó | ries of óld |

The dactyl is long–short–short:

Bríght-est and | bést of the | sóns of the | mórn-ing |

Here the last foot is shortened, in the first and third lines by one syllable, in the second and fourth by two, thus avoiding monotony. A hymn is said to be iambic, anapaestic, trochaic or dactylic after the name of the predominant foot.

This system of measuring verse dates back to Greek and Latin poets. Experiments have been made with other systems for English verse, but the foot system has proved to be the best, especially for lyrics. In adapting it to the peculiarities of our language, three things should be remembered. First, the old terms 'long' and 'short' denote stress, not duration alone. Second, most monosyllablic words can occupy either a stressed or an unstressed position in the metre. Thus the word 'of', short by nature, as in

Is bórn | of Dá | vid's líne |

becomes long by position in

The án | gel óf | the Lórd | came dówn |

where it is stressed just enough to maintain the rhythm. This is known as secondary stress. Third, an English foot normally has one, and only one, stressed syllable.

The amphibrach (short–long–short), associated with the limerick, is rare in hymns. The American, Oman Westendorf, uses it effectively:

> Sent fórth by | God's bléssing | our trúe faith |
> confésssing |
> The peóple | of Gód from | his dwélling | take léave |

The levity of the metre is tempered by internal rhymes (blessing, confessing), by the shortened final foot of alternate lines, and by the apt music of the words themselves. Sung to the haunting Welsh air The Ash Grove, this hymn has an atmosphere of dedicated conviviality which is appropriate after the Eucharist.

The amphibrach more often occurs as a variation from the foot-pattern. The shortening of the final foot is common practice. Thus a dactyl when shortened becomes a trochee and a trochee a monosyllable which, being long, can stand as a whole foot. But when the final syllable of an iambic line is dropped the remaining syllable, being short, cannot stand as a foot. It is therefore added to the preceding foot, which so becomes an amphibrach:

> The dáy | thou gá | vest, Lórd, | is en-ded |

Variations may occur anywhere in a line. As a rule trochees and dactyls work well together:

> Gód is | wórking his | púrpose | oút as | yéar suc | céeds
> to | yéar |

Likewise iambs and anapaests:

> Thou didst léave | thy thróne | and thy kíng | ly crówn |

A beautiful example of variation is sapphic metre, so called after the Greek poetess Sappho (c. 600 BC). It came into Christian hymnody in Latin hymns of about the sixth century. Translations were made in the same metre for EH in 1906 so that they could be sung to their proper plainsong or to the fine French and German melodies written for them in the seventeenth century:

> Fáther, we | práise thee | | nów the | níght is | óver;
> Áctive and | wátchful, | | stánd we | áll be- | fóre thee;
> Sínging, we | óffer | | práyer and | médi- | tátion;
> Thús we a- | dóre thee. (NEH 149)

An important feature is the *caesura*—a pause in the rhythm of a line (marked ||). To fit the old sapphic tunes this pause should follow the fifth syllable of each line and coincide with the sense.

I have dwelt on the subject of metre for four reasons. First, hymns are for singing and metre is rhythm, the common ground on which verse and music meet. Second, metre imparts feeling; it should therefore match the thought. As a tripping metre is alien to serious thought, so a sedate metre would sit ill with the light-hearted mood of, say, 'Give me joy in my heart, keep me praising'. Third, metre, once established, creates a tide of expectancy against which the slightest variation becomes significant. A trochee at the beginning of an iambic line, for instance, can change the atmosphere. Run-on lines heighten tension, especially when combined with caesura. Fourth, an imaginative metre can inspire an imaginative tune, the importance of which we shall see in chapter 8.

Rhyme is not essential to a hymn. 'O come, all ye faithful' has none. Rhyme, however, is desirable because, like metre, it aids the memory; moreover, in the hands of an artist it can give beauty and cohesion to a stanza.

Most rhymes are of one syllable, which is always stressed. In rhymes of two or three syllables the first is stressed. Triple rhyme is usually reserved for light verse. A fine exception is the hymn 'O worship the Lord in the beauty of holiness', in which triple and single rhymes are interlaced, providing a cheerful atmosphere without loss of reverence.

To aid the memory, rhymed lines should be close enough to strike the ear. In LM, rhyming couplets work best. Many CM hymns are rhymed in the second and fourth lines only, giving the effect of the old fourteeners (rhymed lines of fourteen syllables). This form of verse was fashionable in the mid-sixteenth century, the heydey of the English ballad, when our first metrical psalter was in the making. It is reasonable to infer that CM had its origin in the fourteener and was split into eights and sixes for convenience of singing.

Rhyme is by sound rather than sight. In a perfect rhyme all sounds after the first are identical, whatever the spelling. Thus *line* and *sign*, de-*votion* and *ocean*, *tenderness* and *slenderness* are perfect rhymes. Imperfect or off rhymes may be assonance (rhyme of vowels but not consonants—*won* with *sung*, *farthest* with re-*gardest*; consonance (rhyme of consonants but not vowels)—*name* with dia-*dem*; or eye-rhymes (which look right on paper but sound wrong in speech)—*love* with *prove*. Such off rhymes do not necessarily jar on the ear, especially if covered by an intervening line, a run-on, or a caesura. All those examples are from hymns that have stood the test of time.

Eye-rhymes, particularly in old hymns, may be due to change of pronunciation. Milton, for instance, makes *great* rhyme with *seat*. That this passed as a perfect rhyme a century later is attested by Boswell, who quotes Johnson as saying: 'When I published the plan for my Dictionary, Lord Chesterfield told me that the word *great* should be pronounced so as to rhyme to *state*; and Sir William Yonge sent me word that it should be pronounced so as to rhyme to *seat*, and that none but an Irishman would pronounce it *grait*.' That was in 1772, the decade in which William Cowper rhymed *fast* with *taste* and *down* with *own*.

Pronunciation is learnt by ear. Only since radio broadcasting has an approach to uniform pronunciation become feasible. Perfect rhyme is ideal, but a few off rhymes are not sufficient grounds for condemning a hymn that has something important to say.

So far we have considered the basic requirements in any hymn. As an act of *public* worship it must be such as a cross section of the public can readily pick up and sing. As worship, however, it is a human response to the love of God. This calls for appropriate thought, feeling and expression.

The thought should be conducive to worship. A good hymn will fall into one or more of the four categories outlined in chapter 1: to God about God, to God about ourselves, to us about God, to us about ourselves. Even hymns in the last group, though concerned with human life and conduct, usually relate to God at some point. In a good hymn the flow of thought is so natural and logical that such technicalities as rhyme and metre seem incidental.

Feeling is akin to thought and should match it. The relationship is two-way: feeling may generate thought or thought feeling. We have noted the conviction that glows in English hymns of the eighteenth century: Watts, Wesley, Doddridge and Cowper were inspired by a passionate feeling of personal gratitude for the divine love shown in Jesus Christ. John Newton's feeling is never in question: in 'How sweet the name of Jesus sounds' it attains the fire of real poetry; in 'Amazing grace' it shines with an infectious glow, though beyond the author's power of expression. The same impulse of feeling is evident in American hymn-writers of the following century: from Ray Palmer and the poet John Greenleaf Whittier to George Duffield and the associates of Ira Sankey, whereas the feeling of nineteenth-century English hymnists seems to spring rather from their thought. In 1808 James Montgomery was asked by Edward Bickersteth to write a hymn on prayer. The result was what at first sight is a string of statements beginning 'Prayer is the soul's sincere desire' (NEH 442). But as it unfolds, each statement is seen to describe a feeling that prompts prayer. The intensity grows until finally the singer is moved to cry 'Lord, teach us how to pray'.

Expression thus matched to thought engenders feeling. It is not the mere catalogue of feelings that brings the singer to his knees, but the images used to describe them: 'the burden of a sigh', 'the falling of a tear', 'the upward glancing of an eye'; also the poignant contrast between 'the simplest form of speech' and 'the sublimest strains', and again between 'the contrite sinner's voice' and the rejoicing angels' cry 'Behold, he prays!' Such poetic touches go straight to the heart and convey the feeling.

Religious thoughts and feelings, being abstract, are usually expressed in imagery. This may be literal, as in 'All things bright and beautiful'; symbolic, like 'the falling of a tear'; or figurative, as in 'Teach me, my God and King', which we looked at earlier. Pictures from everyday life work well so long as they are familiar. In time, however, the meaning of a word can change. 'Comforter', for instance, when it appeared in a fourteenth-century English bible, meant 'strengthener'—a fair translation of both the Greek and Latin texts of John 14:26. Today it connotes a woolly scarf—which hardly describes the Holy Spirit. Yet the word sticks.

Figures of speech abound in scripture, and it is not always easy to distinguish figure from fact. That our Lord's timing of his crucifixion to coincide with the Jewish Passover season was symbolic he himself attested at the Last Supper: 'This cup is the *new* covenant in *my* blood.' His disciples would readily remember the blood of the paschal lamb sprinkled on their ancestors' doorposts to immunise them in the last plague and release them from bondage. Hence they came to see Jesus as 'the Lamb of God who takes away the sin of the world' (John 1:29) and the Church as 'the Israel of God' (Galatians 6:16). The Church is also called 'the bride, the wife of the Lamb', and 'the holy city, new Jerusalem' (Revelation 21)—hence Salem, Zion and City of God; and Canaan, the promised land, represents the heaven towards which we travel here as 'pilgrims'.

These metaphors occur frequently in hymns and are intelligible to Bible readers; but to a generation for the most part ignorant of scripture, accustomed to taking statements literally, and bombarded daily with news in which Israel is seen as a catalyst for war in the Middle East, they may well present problems. Even the well-known Advent hymn, 'O come, O come, Emmanuel, and ransom captive Israel', may need explanation—or retranslation.

Where there is a risk of misunderstanding, a safer figure of speech is the simile: though less striking than the metaphor, it is more explicit. In 'There is a land of pure delight' Watts has shown how simile can be used with poetic power. The first two verses make it clear that his subject is heaven; the simile, 'death, like a narrow stream', shows that he is speaking figuratively. Then comes the grand simile:

Sweet fields beyond the swelling flood
   Stand dressed in living green:
So to the Jews old Canaan stood
   While Jordan rolled between.

This provides the key to the allusions in the closing verses. Note that the attractive earthly scene captures the imagination before the parallel with Canaan is drawn.

As simile and metaphor can illuminate thought and inspire feeling by comparison of like concepts, antithesis can do it by contrast of opposites, as we saw in Montgomery's hymn on prayer. So also can hyperbole, by exaggeration to the point of impossibility:

> E'en eternity's too short
> to extol thee.

It should be remembered that the purpose of a figure of speech is to clarify. Those examples will suffice to point two principles for their use in hymns. The first is aptness: a far-fetched figure defeats its own object. The second is freshness: the more a particular figure has been used, the less striking it becomes. An apt and striking figure of speech will drive a point home and rivet it in the memory.

Choice of the right words can entertain and win the hearer. A poet savours words like a wine-taster. When their sound is 'an echo to the sense' as Pope puts it, words convey both thought and feeling. George Herbert (in 'Let all the world in every corner sing') achieves this in two lines of apt monosyllables:

> The Church with psalms must shout;
> No door can keep them out.

And consider this stanza from 'The duteous day now closeth', by Robert Bridges:

> Now all the heavenly splendour
> Breaks forth in starlight tender
> From myriads worlds unknown;
> And man the marvel seeing,
> Forgets his selfish being
> For joy of beauty not his own.

Here is unity of thought, feeling and expression. Such word-music not only pleases and persuades; it inspires. Alter a syllable and the magic is lost.

A few observations are called for on the controversial subject of archaisms. They are of two kinds: words no longer in common use and words that have changed their meaning. As to the former, it is argued by some that such words should be altered to save the hymns from going out of use because young people don't understand them. I cannot agree. Words like 'thou', 'thee', 'thine', 'ye', and 'yea' are enshrined in our native poetry and survive in dialects. To alter them muffles the chime of their rich vowel music. To say they are no longer understood is an insult. I have yet to meet a teenager who is puzzled by, say, the new gospel song, 'Seek ye first the kingdom of God'—in which sayings of Christ are quoted from the AV of 1611—or, for that matter, by the old form of the Lord's Prayer. It is one thing to treat God as a friend; quite another to regard him as an equal. To reserve the time-honoured form of address at least for the Almighty could correct this trend. As for the old hymns, let them stand. They are more likely to die of the operation than of their supposed disorder.

Words that have changed their meaning, on the other hand, can be misleading and often harmful, as we noted in the case of 'comforter'. The same is true of 'awful', which now connotes something boring. Words like these damage the faith and should be changed. But let it be done by a poet.

The notion that the general public does not appreciate poetry is false. Consider the popularity of these hymns: 'Let all the world in every corner sing'; 'Teach me, my God and King'; 'When all thy mercies, O my God'; 'God moves in a mysterious way'; 'O for a closer walk with God'; 'Dear Lord and father of mankind'; 'Immortal love for ever full'; 'In the bleak midwinter'; 'All my hope on God is founded'; 'Happy are they, they that love God'; and, of course, Blake's 'Jerusalem'. All these are by great poets. There are also minor poets, like Montgomery, Watts, Newman and Jan Struther, whose hymns we should be sorry to lose. Henry Lyte—author of two of the most famous hymns in the English-speaking world, 'Praise, my soul' and 'Abide with me'—won university prizes for poetry, as did also Heber, Milman, Faber and J.M. Neale; and who would deny the title of poet to Charles Wesley? Poetry can achieve three of the hymn-writer's objects: to kindle the imagination, to aid the memory and to inspire the mind.

In looking at a hymn, then, we shall ask ourselves these questions. Does it achieve its object? To whom is it addressed and what is it about? Is the thought worth preserving? Is it scriptural? Is it expressed clearly and concisely? Does every word do something to the sense or to the feeling? And we shall be on the look-out for poetic touches in the use of metre and imagery and in the choice of words.

Finally we must not forget that a hymn stands or falls by its tune. Music and verse are equal partners. But that is the subject of another chapter.

3 HYMNS TO GOD ABOUT GOD: PRAISE

THE PUREST PRAISE is that addressed directly to God about himself. Some hymns, classified as praise and rightly used as such, like 'All people that on earth do well', 'Praise, my soul, the King of heaven', and the psalms on which they are based, are exhortations addressed to the worshipper. The praise is implicit, as when one speaks highly of one person to another. On the human level, this is considered the higher tribute; but in the worship of God direct praise bespeaks the deeper devotion. It is with such hymns that we are concerned in this chapter.

PRAISE TO THE TRINITY forms our first group. Christian belief begins with faith in one God who has revealed himself to mankind in three ways: 'God in three persons, blessed Trinity'.

Holy! Holy! Holy! Lord God almighty. We have already noted the poetic quality of Reginald Heber's hymns. This is perhaps his greatest, Tennyson thought highly of it. Heber introduced broader and much varied metres into English hymnody. That of 'Holy! Holy! Holy!' is unique. The first line, lifted word for word from the Authorised Version of Revelation 4:8, establishes the rhythm and is immediately followed by an echo of Psalm 63:1. In the next verse our praises are joined with those of the apocalyptic company around the sea of glass and of the cherubim and seraphim in the vision of Isaiah. In the third stanza the glory of God is momentarily obscured by a passing cloud, a reflection on human sin. Another quotation from the bible, this time the Song of Hannah (1 Samuel 2:2), recalls our thoughts to the unique holiness of God, and the full splendour bursts out with renewed intensity in the final verse, when all creation joins in the song. No other hymn so majestically comprehends God's attributes. The Christian is enabled to praise God for being holy, almighty, everlasting, merciful, 'perfect in power, in love and purity', above all, for being the Trinity. Intellectual problems roll away as one sings these lines.

Bright the vision that delighted. One gloomy weekday morning in November, a friend of mine, the vicar of a shrinking, down-town parish, was standing at the altar for the daily celebration. Only one communicant was present, an elderly lady. At the words 'Therefore with angels and archangels ...' he was suddenly overwhelmed with a sense of being surrounded by crowds of worshippers joining in the sanctus. It was, he says, a most vivid experience which he will never forget. As he shook hands with the old lady after the service, she smiled and said, 'Well, we were not alone, were we?' The experience had been shared. No doubt it was known many years before to the author of this hymn, Bishop Richard Mant, who in the first half of the nineteenth century wrote much prose and verse, most of it now forgotten. We should be grateful to him for this reminder of the unseen, unheard company which surrounds us at the Lord's service.

Like the preface and *Sanctus* in the Eucharist, Bishop Mant's hymn is based on Isaiah 6:1–3. Its original four eight-line stanzas are never sung in their entirety. The usual arrangement, in six quatrains, falls naturally into two equal twelve-line sections, each ending with the refrain, 'Lord, thy glory fills the heaven'. Thus we have, as it were, a diptych, each side featuring the *Sanctus*. On the one hand is Isaiah's vision of the worship of heaven; on the other, the Church on earth joins in and thunders the same refrain. This structure can be realised musically still to the tune *Laus Deo*, by singing verses 1 to 3 without a break and adding a descant to verse 3. After a measured pause, verses 4 to 6 may be treated in the same way.

Angel voices ever singing. When the Vicar of Wingate in Lancashire invited his friend Francis Pott, the 28-year-old-curate of Ardingly in Berkshire, to write a festival hymn for the dedication of the new organ at his church, and Edwin George Monk to write the music, his sights were high. Pott had already a number of hymns and translations to his credit and was on the committee of A&M, the first edition of which was about to be published. Monk (no relation to W.H. Monk) had recently been appointed organist of York Minister. Each excelled himself: the resultant hymn 'Angel voices', was duly sung at Wingate in February 1861, became popular and soon found its way into various collections, notably the Supplement to A&M (1889).

'Angel voices' has been a favourite ever since, not only at choir Festivals and recitals, but as a general hymn of praise. It is appropriate at the eucharistic offertory, its theme being that 'craftsman's art and music's measure' represent human work with God's gifts. It does not add that this can be acceptable only when offered through Jesus Christ. Critics might seize on this omission. They might object to the first verse with its celestial-choir-and-harp ensemble, the only scriptural support for which is in two allegorical passages, Revelation 5 and 14. They might also point to one or two careless rhymes. Maybe it was for such reasons that the hymn was dropped in the austere 1904 edition of A&M and excluded from EH (1906). Nevertheless it was soon reinstated in A&M and is now in most Anglican and Free Church hymnals; even EH relented in 1986. It is valuable because it says things that worshippers believe and no other hymn enables them to express. Its metre is unique; Monk's tune matches the words and has a fine climax. In the second verse I see no reason for altering Pott's 'mental eye' to 'mortal eye', still less for changing 'Yea' in the last line of the same verse to the hideously sibilant 'Yes'.

Each generation sees in God what it most needs. Contemporary writers have contributed something new in praise of the Trinity. Patrick Appleford, in a hymn entitled 'Alive for God' (A&M 355, part 1), praises the Father for caring, the Son for bringing forgiveness, and the Holy Spirit for inspiring the Church and feeding its members by prayer and sacrament, and sees in the unity of the Trinity the pattern and potential of unity of nations and races. As originally written for the USPG this hymn's seven stanzas alternated between praise and prayer for social justice. The new arrangement in two parts, praise in part 1 and prayer in part 2, increases its usefulness.

Steward Cross must have written 'Father, Lord of all creation' (A&M 356) with John Robinson's book *Honest to God* in mind: God the Father is 'ground of being', Jesus the 'man for others', and the Holy Ghost 'God in us'. Particularly invigorating is the stirring scriptural ascription to the Holy Spirit in verse 3:

> Holy Spirit, rushing, burning
> wind and flame of Pentecost.

There are lines of supplication in verses 2 and 3, but the predominant mood is praise.

Christopher Idle has given us metrical settings of the early Trinitarian canticles, *Gloria in excelsis* and *Te Deum*: the former, 'Glory in the highest to the God of heaven!' (HTC 582, NEH 363), in rhyming trochaic couplets set to the tune Cuddesdon by W.H. Ferguson; the latter, 'God, we praise you!' (HTC 341), to Parry's tune Rustington. Metre and rhyme, as I have already suggested, have distinct advantages as regards congregational singing. Here the author has skilfully succeeded in presenting these ancient songs in memorable modern English verse without padding on the one hand or loss of any essential feature on the other.

Father, we adore you (MP 44)—words and music by Terrye Coelho (1972)—has three remarkable features: its pattern—three three-line verses, so symbolising the Trinity; its economy—a twelve-word refrain prefaced by Father (verse 1), Jesus (verse 2), Spirit (verse 3), making fifteen words in all; and its tune which, sung as a three-part round as suggested, symbolises the unity of the Trinity while obviating the tedium of repetition. Thus we approach the greatest mystery of our religion with adoration, self-dedication and sincerity. What could be simpler? Yet it says all.

PRAISE TO GOD THE FATHER makes up the next group. In their preface to the 1904 edition of A&M the editors deplore the lack of hymns addressed to God the Father. This defect, they say, 'lies largely with the composers of our hymns and not with the compilers of the collections'. Two years later Percy Dearmer, with characteristic impishness, included in EH two fine hymns of praise to God: 'Immortal, invisible, God only wise', which had then been published for nearly forty years, and 'How shall I sing that majesty', which had been in print since 1683. Dearmer thus made his point that such hymns, though rare, had been there all the time ready for the picking, but compilers had not cast their nets widely enough.

When all thy mercies, O my God. The author, Joseph Addison, the famous literary layman of the Augustan age, was no theologian. Like his other hymns, this is entirely Old Testament in thought and content. Appended to an essay on gratitude in the *Spectator* (1712), it expresses in elegant verse a plain man's faith in God's providence. Addison's phrase in his first stanza, 'lost in wonder, love and praise', was used by Charles Wesley as the climax of his hymn, 'Love divine, all loves excelling' in 1747. Such petty plagiarism was common in the eighteenth century. Addison himself in his last stanza has lifted the conceit, 'eternity's too short', from George Herbert's 'King of glory, King of peace', which was published in 1633. It is only fair to add that, as the Metaphysical poets had gone out of fashion by the dawn of the eighteenth century, Addison may not have come across Herbert's hymn. There is, however, no doubt that the Wesleys knew Addison's 'When all thy mercies', for they included it in their first Collection of 1737.

My God, how wonderful thou art. Frederick William Faber (1814–63), brought up and ordained in the Church of England, was, like Heber, a Newdigate prizeman at Oxford. At the age of 32 he became a Roman Catholic and set himself to do for that Church what the Wesleys had done for Methodists and Cowper and Newton for Anglicans. With them as his models, Faber wrote 150 hymns with—as he states in his preface—'a double end in view: first to furnish some simple hymns for singing; secondly to provide English Catholics with a hymn book for reading, in the simplest and least involved metres; both these objects have not infrequently required considerable sacrifice in a literary point of view.' His critics should bear this in mind.

This much loved hymn of adoration, addressed to God, not only for his majesty, beauty and awesomeness, but also for his love and forbearance, deserves its place today in hymnals of all denominations. As it has been amply discussed elsewhere I need only to add that the final verse—'What rapture will it be Prostrate before thy throne to lie And gaze and gaze on thee!'—is a poetic overstatement and need not be taken literally.

O worship the King. The theme of Psalm 104, one of

scripture's most majestic outpourings of praise, is the providence of God. Providence is a combination of power and love, each of which in God is perfect, therefore his providence is unlimited. Upon this psalm Sir Robert Grant, barrister, politician and from 1834 Governor of Bombay, founded his hymn 'O worship the King'. Most of the psalm is addressed to the worshipper about God, there being only four verses in which God is addressed directly. The frequent and apparently arbitrary changes of person which abound in the psalter can be bewildering. The hymn is much tidier in construction, switching to the second person in verse 3 and continuing so to the end. It therefore qualifies for inclusion among hymns addressed to God about God.

Paraphrases of the Psalms are usually less distinguished than the Prayer Book version. Grant has managed to give to his lines a distinction of their own. 'Thou art clothed with majesty and honour' becomes:

> Pavilioned in splendour
>   And girded with praise.

And Coverdale's nineteen words in verse 2, 'Thou deckest thyself with light as it were with a garment: and spreadest out the heavens like a curtain' are epitomised in two pithy phrases:

> Whose robe is the light,
>   Whose canopy space.

The next four lines are based on verse 3 of the psalm, with the thunder borrowed from verse 7 to add a touch of awe. The rest of the hymn is a free exposition of thoughts which this great psalm of nature suggests. Our scientific age tends to regard creation with less wonder than in the past; Grant, however, cites three elements essential to man's existence which man himself cannot create—air, light and water—as expressions of that 'measureless might, ineffable love' which are combined in the providence of God.

Lord of the boundless curves of space. The twentieth century challenges hymn-writers to depict God as lord not only of primeval nature but also of the universe that modern science has revealed. Albert Bayly has taken up the challenge.

The words 'galaxy', 'cell' and 'atom', and old words with new connotations like 'space', 'time' and 'energy', are seen as partners in the quest for truth. Complementary to this is the prayer-hymn, 'O Lord of every shining constellation', by the same author. Such language in a hymn-book must have strengthened 'the uneasy truce between science and theology' (John Habgood's phrase in *Soundings*, 1962).

PRAISE TO GOD THE SON is the next category. Christian theology is founded on the unique life and personality of Jesus, recorded in the Gospels and claimed by the apostles to be divine. It is not surprising, therefore, that from earliest times hymns of praise have been addressed to him in terms of human affection.

Hail, gladdening light. We have already noted the early origin of the Greek evening hymn, *Phos hilaron*, of which this translation by Keble in A&M is the best known. It is a sublime hymn of praise to Christ, , the light of the world. EH gives Robert Bridges's fine version, 'O gladsome light, O grace'; but the gain in poetic grace is offset by a loss in force and appeal. Bridges is near the Greek in his line 'We see the evening light'; Longfellow's version of this hymn in *The Golden Legend* had 'And seeing the evening twilight'. But the occasion of its singing was 'the lighting of lamps', and I must confess a preference for Keble's 'The lights of evening round us shine', which suggests lamps appearing in streets and windows at dusk. A simpler translation, beginning 'O Brightness of the eternal Father's face', made by E.W. Eddis in 1863 and later included by SPCK in *Church Hymns*, has the graphic lines:

> Now that the daylight fades, and one by one
> The lamps of evening shine:

It is worth reviving, not least for the tune *Lux vera*, composed expressly for it by Dykes, and one of his best.

Jesu, the very thought ... The Latin hymn, *Jesus dulcis memoria*, owes much of its popularity with English-speaking people partly to the belief that it was the work of St Bernard, the great twelfth-century Abbot of Clairvaux, and partly to the translation by Edward Caswall. The hymn, however, is now thought to be of English origin, though the author's name has not been traced. As for Caswall's translation:

> Jesu, the very thought of thee
>   With sweetness fills the breast;
> But sweeter far thy face to see
>   And in thy presence rest—

there is a streak of sentimentality in the poem, and Caswall has exaggerated it. J.M. Neale's version is stronger, and nearer to the rhythm and feeling of the Latin:

> Jesu! the very thought is sweet!
>   In that dear name all heart-joys meet;
> But sweeter than the honey far
>   The glimpses of his presence are.

Dulcis in classical Latin means 'sweet to the taste' and, in a figurative sense, 'delightful to the senses'. When applied to persons, however, it carries the meaning 'dear', 'kind', 'friendly'. In this sense Cicero wrote '*optime et dulcissime frater*' – 'best and dearest brother'. The corresponding Greek word *glukus* (from which we get 'glucose') is used of persons in the same way. This figurative sense was understood when the hymns were written. Moreover, the play on the two senses of *dulcis* in the first stanza of *Jesus dulcis memoria*, lost in English translations, would have been appreciated in the Middle Ages:

> *sed super mel et omnia*
> *eius dulcis praesentia.*

The unfortunate prevalence of the epithet 'sweet' applied to our Lord in hymns of the nineteenth century has helped us to create a false image repellent to the modern mind.

The difficulty of rendering Latin verse in suitable English verse has already been referred to in Chapter 1. The main problem is that Latin words are generally long and their English equivalents short; moreover, extra words—pronouns, prepositions, auxiliary verbs, and so on—are used in English to convey what in Latin is often represented by inflections. This gives the Latin more punch. For example, no English translation can convey the epigrammatic force of:

nil canitur sauvius,
nil auditur jucundius,
nil cogitatur dulcius,
quam Jesus Dei filius.

Thirteen words. Neale has to use twenty-nine, of which eleven (here given in italics) are makeweights:

No *word* is sung more sweet *than this*:
No *name* is heard more *full of* bliss:
No thought *brings* sweeter *comfort nigh*,
Than Jesus, Son of God *most high*.

In appraising these hymns of the ancient Church, therefore, it must be remembered that they cannot be judged fairly by their English versions. Neither must we be too critical of their translators, who rather deserve our gratitude for the difficult task they have accomplished so well. If we cannot visit Venice, at least we may catch some of its magic from a Canaletto.

Jesu, thou joy of loving hearts. It is true to say that this hymn would never have been written but for *Jesus dulcis memoria*. Yet it is not a translation; rather it might be called a nineteenth-century descendant. Ray Palmer (1808–87), its author, was an American Congregational minister. His method was to select five verses from the Latin poem and meditate upon them. The result is a strong, modern hymn of praise to Christ, without trace of sentimentality yet warm in its devotion. Though suitable for general use, it is most appropriate at the Eucharist. Singing it, the worshipper finds in Christ, and especially in the sacrament of his presence, 'that peace which the world cannot give'. The final verse sums up the meaning of the hymn. It is because of human sin that man finds himself groping in darkness; once the light of Christ has dispelled this darkness, life, though perhaps still outwardly turbulent, becomes inwardly serene.

Jesus, these eyes have never seen. This hymn too is by Ray Palmer, expressing his own personal devotion to Christ. 'He was preparing a sermon which had Christ for its special theme. Needing a volume from his closed book-case, he rose and opened the door, when the book appeared first in his hand. At once it occurred to him that in some such way the face of Christ would be unveiled to us: and the thought so filled his heart that he turned to his desk and composed the hymn.' This is Dr Duffield's account as he claims to have received it from the author himself. Many people today, while prepared to accept the fact of the historical Jesus, find difficulty in sensing his presence as a real person. This hymn should help them.

How sweet the name of Jesus sounds. It is the sound of the name that is sweet, not Jesus himself. The idea is from the Song of Songs 1:3: 'Thy name is as ointment poured forth.' The hymn, as usually sung, falls into three sections of two verses each. The first section quietly expands the initial thought. But verse 3 starts like a clap of thunder: "Dear name!" John Newton then pours forth a torrent of that passionate personal devotion to which I have already referred. But note how, even in his flight of fervour, Newton keeps within the bounds of scripture. 'Rock', 'shield' and 'hiding-place' are designations of God in Psalms; to give them to Christ is to declare his divinity. As for 'boundless stores of grace', nobody will need reminding of the sublime cadence of the Christmas Gospel, 'full of grace and truth' (John 1:14). Nor is the passion spent. In verse 4, addressed to Christ himself, its intensity reaches the point of incandescence:

> Jesus, my shepherd, husband, friend,
> My prophet, priest and king,
> My Lord, my life, my way, my end,
> Accept the praise I bring.

Such a procession of titles must be unique in hymnody. Yet all ten are from the New Testament. Jesus said, 'I am the good *shepherd*') (John 10:14); since the Church is metaphorically the Bride of Christ (Mark 2:19, Ephesians 5:23, Revelation 19 etc.) its members can look to him as '*husband*'; Jesus is also '*friend* of sinners' (Matthew 11:19), '*prophet* of Nazareth' (Matthew 21:11), 'a high *priest* for ever' (Hebrews 6:20), '*King*' (Luke 19:38), '*Lord*' (John 20:28), 'the *way*, the truth and the *life*' (John 14:6) and, in the apocalyptic vision, 'the beginning and the *end*' (Revelation 21:6). The closing section, still addressed to Christ, is calm, and ends with a prayer which must voice the silent hope of all believers:

> And may the music of thy name
> Refresh my soul in death.

King of glory, King of peace, offers two more scriptural titles. George Herbert (1593–1633), scholar-poet-musician, having distinguished himself at Cambridge and at the court of King James I, decided, at the age of 36, to offer himself for ordination and became Rector of Bemerton near Salisbury, where he spent the last three years of his life. It was there that he wrote *The Temple*, a collection of some 160 religious poems and lyrics. This manuscript Herbert, on his death-bed, handed to his friend Nicholas Ferrar. It was immediately published. The author could hardly have imagined that three centuries later four of his lyrics would be known and loved as hymns by all English-speaking Christians: 'The God of love my shepherd is'; 'Teach me, my God and King'; 'Let all the world in every corner sing'; and 'King of glory, King of peace'. The last had to wait until the present century to be included in a hymn book. Its mood is that of the publican in the parable who beat his breast and said, 'God be merciful unto me a sinner', and went home with his prayer answered. 'I will move thee', sings Herbert, confident of God's compassion.

Originally 'King of glory, King of peace' had seven quatrains in the then unusual metre of 7474, which may be the reason why its potential as a hymn was for so long overlooked. The order of these verses is typical of Herbert's tidy thinking: verses 1, 3 and 5 are direct praise, 2, 4 and 6, also addressed to God, give the reason for the praise. Thus the short lines of the odd verses begin with 'I', those of the even verses with 'Thou', and verse 7 rounds off the song. But the sibilant sixth stanza has never been sung as part of a hymn:

> Thou grew'st soft and moist with tears,
> Thou relented'st,
> And when justice call'd for fears,
> Thou dissented'st.

Leaving out these line breaks the 'I' – 'Thou' sequence, which Herbert clearly intended as a feature. Yet the form in which the poem is sung today—three eight-line verses—improves it as a hymn.

Thine be the glory (AM 428, NEH 120). In these verses, written in French in 1884, a Swiss pastor takes us personally to the empty tomb and introduces us to the risen Master. This and Dearmer's 'A brighter dawn is breaking' (NEH 102) are the only two well-known Easter hymns of praise addressed to Christ.

It is worth drawing attention to three important hymns by modern writers. **To mock your reign** (A&M 517), an inspired Passiontide hymn by Fred Pratt Green, is an exposition of our Lord's words from the cross, 'Father, forgive them; for they know not what they do.' To sing these thought-provoking verses, particularly to Tallis' Third Mode Melody, for which they were written, is a deeply moving experience.

O Christ the same through all our story's pages, by Bishop Timothy Dudley-Smith, appeared first in HTC (263) in 1982 and four years later in NEH (258). In the latter it is set to the Londonderry Air, which fits it perfectly and has the advantage of being well known. This hymn, based on Hebrews 13:8—'Jesus Christ the same, yesterday, today and for ever' is, I think, the only one of direct praise to Christ for this assurance; indeed, it is the New Testament counterpart of Watt's version of Psalm 90, 'O God, our help'.

All I once held dear is one of Graham Kendrick's songs, published by Make Way in 1993. Words and tune are in the home-spun style he had made his own. Like it or not, the important thing is what it says, based on St Paul's famous declaration of commitment to Christ at Philippians 3:7–11. It is a timely message to this age, obsessed as it is with wordly values. Those who can sing this song with the author's sincerity have got their priorities right.

PRAISE TO GOD THE HOLY SPIRIT comes next. It is remarkable that, almost without exception, hymns addressed to the Holy Spirit are prayers. Hymns of praise to the Holy Spirit are practically non-existent: before 1900 only one was in common use, 'To thee, O Comforter divine', by Frances Ridley Havergal (A&M 1875 no. 212). It is an undistinguished jingle of Victorian clichés, but at least it enabled our grandparents to address their praises to the Holy Spirit personally.

O Holy Spirit, God (SP 601). Percy Dearmer, the author, tells us that it was written 'in order to provide a hymn which children could sing, and which should touch on other aspects of the working of the Eternal Spirit, as well as those enumerated in the Whitsuntide hymns'. There is a streak of pantheism in some of Dearmer's later writings, but the statements contained in these colourful and refreshing verses all seem to be reasonable deductions from what the Bible teaches about the Spirit of God. It has the virtue of portraying 'the Lord', the giver of life' as an attractive and lovable person. It is all praise except the final stanza, which is a prayer for three of the Pauline fruits of the Spirit (Galatians 5:22) and four of the Spirit's gifts from Isaiah 11:2.

Hail, blest Spirit, Lord eternal. In the *BBC Hymn Book* (1951) appeared this Whit Sunday processional by one of the Cowley Fathers, Sidney James Wallis. It is well written, embodies in its nine verses much Bible teaching, and is addressed throughout to the Holy Ghost.

Holy Spirit, ever dwelling, written in 1922 for the *Mirfield Mission Hymn Book* by Timothy Rees, afterwards Bishop of Llandaff, deserves mention. All direct praise, it is the only hymn I know which acknowledges the involvement of the third person of the Trinity in the Eucharist:

> Holy Spirit, ever working
> Through the Church's ministry—
> Quick'ning, strength'ning and absolving,
> Setting captive sinners free:
> Holy Spirit, consecrating
> Every Eucharist on earth,
> Unto thee be endless praises
> For thy gifts of endless worth.

Considering the gap it fills, it is surprising that this hymn is not more widely published. *With One Voice* (1979) and the

New EH (1986) include it, but much edited, and omitting the lines about the Eucharist.

To thee, Holy Spirit, lifebreath eternal. In view of the shortage of such hymns, perhaps I may be excused for introducing one written at my request by Gilbert Hudson, a poetic friend, in 1946, to carry Bach's stirring melody, *Dir, dir Jehova.* This is the last verse:

O lifegiver, leader, cleanser, enlight'ner,
Advocate, pleading Christ's cause in our hearts,
Unless by thee hallowed, ne'ere will our worship
Hallow our world-work, our talents, our arts.
Come, fill with thy life all we do or intend,
So shall we the kingdom serve which hath no end.

Except for the prayer in the final couplet the whole hymn is praise to the Holy Spirit for inspiring the prophets and singers of the Old Testament, the apostles of the New, and every worthwhile achievement in the world today.

THE BIBLE AND THE CHURCH supply the final groups in this chapter. Lack of direct praise to the Holy Spirit is to some extent redressed by hymns of thanksgiving for outward and visible signs of the Holy Spirit's activity: the Bible and the Church. Among good modern hymns of thanksgiving for the bible are 'Thanks to God, whose word was spoken' (R.T. Brooks); 'God has spoken by his prophets' (G.W. Briggs); 'The prophets spoke in days of old' (J.E. Bowers); 'God, who has caused to be written for our learning' (H.O'Driscoll); and, for the Gospel, the useful gradual 'Rise and hear! The Lord is speaking (H.C.A. Gaunt).

The Church is seen by St Paul as the Body of Christ, inhabited by the Holy Sprit and therefore to be held in veneration. In Christian worship, the terms Jerusalem, Sion, and City of God are synonymous with the Church, whether on earth or in heaven.

O thou not made with hands. Francis Turner Palgrave in 1867 entitled this hymn 'Kingdom of God within'. It is addressed to the Church—not the building, 'made with hands', but the family of God. In his own words, and order, the poet outlines the nine virtues listed by St Paul as the fruits of the Spirit (Galatians 5:22,23). These are the true signs of the Church—

More bright than gold or gem,
God's own Jerusalem!

Glorious things of thee are spoken. Another hymn of praise, addressed to the Church as 'Sion, city of our God'. John Newton, who was not given to unrestrained jubilation, here lets himself go. The first two lines spring from Psalm 87:3 (AV). Thereafter he draws on ideas from Isaiah 33:20–22. This hymn is valuable for its insistence on the visible nature of the Church as an organic society, membership of which is not contractual but by birth, or rather rebirth in baptism:

Saviour, if of Sion's city
I through grace, a member am ...

The chief privileges of membership are salvation in the New Testament sense (verse 1) and grace (verse 2, where the author clearly has in mind John 4:14). Unlike 'the worlding's pleasure', which fades, these 'solid joys' are eternal. Of the original five verses the three given in EH are the best.

Thy hand, O God, has guided. The Church has its detractors today, as it had over a century ago when E.H. Plumptre wrote this hymn of praise to God for his Church. It reminds us that the Church is both human and divine. Though hindered by the weakness of its human element, it is part of God's creative plan and therefore its ultimate unity and victory are assured.

City of God, how broad and far. Samuel Johnson (1822–82), the American Unitarian (not to be confused with the great English lexicographer of the same name in the previous century), included this in his *Hymns of the Spirit* (1862). It is addressed to the Church itself and dwells, like Newton's 'Glorious things', on its permanence and impregnability. Certain cynics have denounced this hymn as a monstrous piece of wishful thinking. Its optimism, however, is justified by our Lord's promise to the Church that the gates of hell shall not prevail against it. The final couplet,

Unharmed upon the eternal rock
The eternal city stands,

may have been intended by Johnson, as a Unitarian, in the Old Testament sense. But to Christians who sing these lines today, 'That rock is Christ', as St Paul says.

The day thou gavest, Lord, is ended. Evening hymn? Missionary hymn? Hymn about the Church? All three, in fact. The first verse makes it appropriate in the evening. Among evening hymns it is unique in its assumption that the world is round and that as one continent's worship ends, another's begins. The subject of this hymn is the world-wide Church, John Ellerton wrote it in 1870 for *A Liturgy for Missionary Meetings*; the following year he included it in the 'Evening' section of *Church Hymns*, of which he was co-editor. In Queen Victoria's Diamond Jubilee celebrations it was sung at thanksgiving services all over the world. At that time the British Empire was at its zenith, and was said to be one on which the sun never set. This hymn reminds us that the same is true of the Church. But whereas 'Earth's proud empires pass away', the Church, despite setbacks, 'stands and grows for ever'.

For all the saints who from their labours rest. This hymn is addressed to Christ in praise of the Church. It was written in 1864 by Bishop Walsham How. Originally it had eleven verses and began 'For all thy saints'. But the present version in eight verses, which the Bishop later preferred, divides naturally into three sections corresponding to the three states of the Church. The first (verses 1, 2 and 3) refers to the Church militant here on earth, confessing faith in Christ, counting on his presence and power, and looking to him as 'captain' and 'one true light' in times of doubt and darkness.

The middle verses (4, 5, and 6) are about the Church expectant.'Paradise' was originally a Persian word for park or garden: hence its association with the Garden of Eden. The same meaning also applies to the intermediate state between death and resurrection, in which the soul, released from the temptation and pressures of this fallen world, may go over the lessons of life, meet Christ (as he promises the penitent thief) and prepare for heaven. This hymn describes it as a state of 'fellowship divine' (verse 4), peace and calm (verse 6) and joy (verse 5), the sound of which occasionally touches the consciousness of those on earth, encouraging them to continue the struggle. And the hymn's last section (verse 7 and 8) pictures the Church triumphant entering heaven at the final resurrection: 'The saints triumphant rise in bright array'. Leading the vast column, we glimpse the King of glory. As the procession unfolds, the world-wide splendour of the Church is revealed, singing in praise of the Trinity.

4 HYMNS TO GOD ABOUT OURSELVES: PRAYER

IT WAS A BITTER, BLACK, STORMY NIGHT about the turn of the century. A homeward-bound British merchant ship, off course near the Irish coast, was battling with a severe storm. Waves beetling like cliffs swept the deck and cascaded into the hold; timbers creaked and split; at any moment, it seemed, the ship would be broken up. The crew lost hope and huddled together, waiting for the end. Somebody called out: 'Does anyone know how to pray?' Presently above the roar of the tempest a clear tenor voice was heard singing 'Eternal Father, strong to save'. It was the youngest member of the crew, a lad of eighteen years, who had been a choirboy and knew the hymn by heart. One by one, others began to join in. When the hymn was finished spirits revived, hope was restored, the men returned to their posts, and after a long struggle the ship was safely berthed in Liverpool.

I have told this story as it was recounted to me years ago by an eyewitness. I have told it because it demonstrates two things: the advantage of singing in a church choir and the value of hymns as a means not only of praising God, but also of knowing him and praying to him. In that storm sermons and Bible stories were forgotten; but the hymn and its teaching were remembered. Nobody on board that ship could frame a prayer; but in the moment of crisis the familiar words and tune rose to the lad's lips and provided a prayer in which others could join.

PRAYER TO GOD IN TRINITY opens this chapter. **Eternal Father, strong to save:** William Whiting, Master of the Quirister School at Winchester College, wrote this famous hymn in 1860. The following year it was revised for inclusion in A&M. The author's own revision appeared in *Church Hymns* (1871) and EH (1906). Whiting's original began thus:

O Thou who biddest the ocean deep
Its own appointed limits keep,

Thou who didst bind the restless wave,
Eternal Father, strong be save,
O hear us ...

The most important change was the promotion of the fourth line to the beginning of the hymn. This is an undoubted improvement, providing a more distinguished title-line and bringing the first verse into line with the second and third, which follow the pattern of the Litany. We have already noted that besides being a prayer, this hymn contains much Bible teaching. This is given in the lines between the invocation and the prayer: in verse 1 it is from Psalm 104:9 and Genesis 1:9; in the second from Mark 4:39 and 6:48; and in the third from Genesis 1:2. The fourth verse breaks this pattern. After invocation of the Trinity, the prayer occupies the next three lines and the final couplet turns to praise.

A straightforward hymn, indissolubly bound with Dykes' equally straightforward tune, 'Eternal Father' has for over a century voiced the simple, down-to-earth faith of the plain man. It will be remembered as one of the three hymns chosen by Sir Winston Churchill to be sung at that historic service on the quarterdeck of HMS *Prince of Wales* on Sunday morning, 10 August 1941, two days before the signing of the Atlantic Charter with President Roosevelt.

Whiting was not the first to use this pattern in addressing the Trinity. Edward Cooper's 'Father of heaven, whose love profound' (1805), based on the first four suffrages of Cranmer's Litany, is similar in form. So is John Marriott's missionary hymn, 'Thou whose almighty word', with its powerful refrain 'Let there be light'. In singing such hymns it should not be forgotten that God is a God of infinite power, wisdom and goodness (Article One). the three Persons are revelations of God, not to be regarded as departmental managers.

Our Father, by whose name (A&M 505). The American F. Bland Tucker has given us this prayer for love and unity in the family based on the love and unity of the Trinity.

PRAYER TO GOD THE FATHER, like all prayers to God, is founded on the assumption that he is eternal, unchanging and boundless in power—otherwise prayer would be profitless; also that, in contrast, man's power is limited and human life and achievement transitory—else prayer would be needless. Such is the theme of Psalm 90, and of the famous hymn based on it by Isaac Watts: **Our God, our help in ages past.** That is what Watts wrote. 'Our' was altered to 'O' by Wesley in 1737. Watts divided Psalm 90 into three sections, the first of which (verses 1 to 6) gives him nine stanzas. It is from these that our hymn has been taken.

For the most part the psalmist's statements are followed phrase by phrase; but now and again Watts breaks loose and gives play to his imagination. Thus 'Lord, thou hast been our refuge: from one generation to another' is paraphrased in the well-known opening couplet. The word *refuge*, however, sparks a train of ideas—*shelter*, *eternal home*, the abode of *saints* and *our defence*—which keeps Watts going for another six lines. It is touches like this that have made the hymn great.

Most of Watt's life was clouded by illness. That may account for an unevenness of quality which is evident sometimes from one verse to another. I imagine it was on one of his off days that he paraphrased verse 15 in the lines:

> Return, O God of love! return,
> Earth is a tiresome place.

Even the sublimity of Watt's first three stanzas is followed by a dubious rhyme:

> Thy word commands our flesh to dust,
> 'Return, ye sons of men';
> All nations rose from earth at first,
> And turn to earth again.

And his sixth stanza, retained in *The Methodist Hymn Book*,

> The busy tribes of flesh and blood,
> With all their lives and cares,
> Are carried downward by the flood,
> And lost in the following years,

says nothing more than is better expressed in his seventh, beginning 'Time, like an ever-rolling stream'. No hymnal has included his eighth stanza:

> Like flowery fields the nations stand,
> Pleased with the morning light:
> The flowers beneath the mower's hand
> Lie withering ere 'tis night.

Watts is not at his best here: a pity, because the psalmist's imagery applied to nations makes the point, attested by history, that all human attempts to govern have failed. The last stanza—which is the first recast as a prayer—rounds off the section and makes it a hymn in itself.

In this paraphrase Watts seems to have departed from his avowed intention to christianise the Psalter. There is not a line that David himself could not have sung. This is a hymn in which Jews and Moslems, as well as Christians, might join unreservedly. It is among the most complete and lasting expressions of devotion in the English language. One cannot envisage an age when it will not be relevant.

O God of Bethel, by whose hand. Perhaps the A&M version beginning 'O God of Jacob' is more explicit. This is another prayer-hymn on the same subject and in the same metre as 'O God, our help'. It is by Philip Doddridge, also a Dissenter, who, though a generation younger, survived Watts by only three years. From Doddridge's first manuscript (dated 1736–7) to the version in *Scottish Paraphrases* (revised 1781) many alterations were made to the text, some by Doddridge himself, others by John Logan (born 1748). The final version is undoubtedly an improvement on the original; but the hymn is essentially by Doddridge. It is based on Genesis 28:20–22. After his dream at Bethel, Jacob, a bargainer by nature, made a bargain with God. If God would look after him in his wanderings and bring him safely home, he would worship him and sacrifice a tenth of his wealth. This hymn puts Jacob's prayer into the mouths of modern singers. In the first manuscript the idea of a bargain is clearly conveyed by the fact that the third and fourth verses begin with an 'If' and the fifth and final verse is a promise:

> To Thee as to our covenant God
> We'll our whole selves reign,

And count that not our tenth alone
But all we have is thine.

In our version, without the 'ifs' and without the promise, the hymn is simply a prayer for God's continuous guidance and providence in all the vicissitudes of life.

Have we not perhaps lost something here? It is easy to laugh at Jacob's primitive presumption in making his bargain with God, but it does at least show a sense of obligation which is lacking in our day. In return for God's blessings, Jacob promised to worship and to tithe his wealth. These are the very things people generally are most reluctant to do. It tends to be forgotten that the Christian, too, has a covenant with God: 'a new covenant in my blood', said Jesus at the institution of the Eucharist, and then he commanded, 'do this.' The purpose of the covenant is to preserve man's free will. Salvation is not forced upon us; it is channelled through sacraments, which we can either take or leave. Likewise we are free in the disposal of our wealth.

Father, hear the prayer we offer. It is one thing to say to God, 'If you will protect me, I will tithe my earnings and worship you': quite another thing to expect that a regular worshipper who tries to live a Christian life has the right to expect immunity from trouble. Neither the Old Testament nor the New supports that view. Trials are there and have to be met; the darkest valley, even death itself, has to be faced. The reward of our religion is the power to cope triumphantly. That is the subject of this hymn by Love Maria Willis. It was made known in America by inclusion in *Hymns of the Spirit*, a notable collection compiled in 1864 by two Americans who had met at Harvard University: Samuel Longfellow (brother of the poet) and Samuel Johnson. The literary quality of the hymn has been much improved, probably by Longfellow, but the subject and thoughts are those of Mrs Willis. Serenity in time of stress is a need we all share.

That may account for the popularity of our next hymn, also from America: **Dear Lord and Father of mankind.** Whittier would be surprised to hear these verses sung with such fervour in churches today. Likewise not a few church people may be surprised to learn that what Whittier meant as he wrote these words and what we mean when we sing them are two very different things. The hymn we know as 'Dear Lord and Father' is a cento, consisting of five of the last six stanzas of a poem entitled 'The Brewing of Soma', in which Whittier describes the ancient heathen rite of drinking the intoxicating Indian soma as a stimulant to worship. The effect was ecstatic frenzy, followed by a peace which was considered to be the god's gift in return for worship. One stanza runs thus:

> Then knew each rapt inebriate
> A winged and glorious birth,
> Soared upward, with strange joy elate,
> Beat, with dazed head, Varuna's gate,
> And, sobered, sank to earth.

This Whittier likens to the use of music and other exciting arts in the worship of the Church:

> And yet the past comes round again,
> And new doth old fulfil;
> In sensual transports wild as vain,
> We brew in many a Christian fane
> The heathen Soma still!

Then follows the first of the five familiar stanzas of the hymn. To the Quaker, Whittier, 'our foolish ways' are the music and ritual of church services and 'our rightful mind' the silence of the Friend's Meeting. The Quakers' lofty concept of silent worship and holy living is epitomised in the two lines:

> In purer lives thy service find,
> In deeper reverence praise.

Thus the very fact of these words being sung is ironic. The forms of our worship are largely a matter of temperament. Not many people feel capable of the intense concentration necessary to express themselves corporately without the use of externals. Nevertheless the Quakers have a point here: although most of us are convinced that music and symbolic ceremonial are valuable aids, there can be no doubt that silence has its place too, especially before and after prayer. As sung and understood today, these five verses are a prayer for the peace of God, that inner serenity amid the strains and pressures of life, for the need of which so many break down in health.

Parry's fine melody, which in recent years has played no small part in popularising this hymn, was never intended as a hymn-tune. In *Judith*, one of his long-forgotten oratorios, is a ballad in which a story is told to a child. A music-master at Repton School observed the remarkable aptness of its melody to these words and set it to them with immediate success (which is why the hymn-tune is called Repton). Thus both words and music are inspired adaptations.

Guide me, O thou great Jehovah. William Williams (1717–91) was converted early in life, ordained, and became a noted itinerant preacher, a poet and a prolific writer of hymns. He might be called the Wesley of Wales. He wrote this hymn—in Welsh, like most of his verse—when he was 28. Of the original five stanzas, the three we sing in English today are 1, 3 and 4: the first from a translation by Peter Williams (no relation), of which the author approved, the other two by William Williams himself. The result is a great hymn based on the Bible narrative of Israel's adventures in the wilderness. To appreciate it one should read Exodus 16 before the first stanza, Exodus 17:1–7 and 13:20–22 before the second, and Joshua 3 before the last. The hymn voices the plain person's basic faith in God's providence in life, in death and beyond it.

Be Thou my guardian and my guide. Isaac Williams, also Welsh though educated in England, was an accomplished Oxford scholar, influenced by Newman and Keble, each of whom in succession he served as curate. In 1842 he published his *Hymns on the Catechism*. To illustrate 'Lead us not into temptation' he wrote these verses. The phraseology of the Lord's prayer at this point has caused many to ask 'Does God lead us into temptation?' No such problem arises from singing this hymn, which is clearly a prayer for strength in temptation.

For the healing of the nations. Fred Kaan, doughty champion of human rights, has recently provided this prayer for grace to abolish from God's world 'all that kills abundant living'. It is a hymn which people of other faiths might sing with Christians.

PRAYER TO GOD THE SON is our next category. **Lord Jesus, think on me.** This Greek hymn by Bishop Synesius, who died c. 430 AD, is probably the earliest Christian prayer-hymn still in use. It began with a fine ascription to Christ, Son of God, and ended with a doxology. These are omitted in our English version, made by Dr A.W. Chatfield in about 1876. The author admits that he has not followed the Greek exactly. However, he has given us a serviceable Lenten hymn. The four verses in A&M are the best. A closer translation, beginning 'Christ, the Son of God most high', was made by Isaac Williams in *Thoughts in Past Years* (1838).

Jesu, lover of my soul. Under the heading 'In time of danger and temptation', this great hymn appeared in 1740, two years after the Wesley brothers had had their conversion experience. It reflects the warming of heart and sense of direction which marked this turning-point in their lives. If we take the hymn as Charles Wesley wrote it (except for a verse that has always been omitted) we shall find that the mainspring is St Paul's doctrine of justification by faith in Christ alone. It is this conviction which shines through such lines as 'Other refuge have I none', 'All my trust on thee is stayed' and 'Thou, O Christ, art all I want'. We shall also see in that puzzling line about 'the nearer waters' an allusion to the inner struggles and uncertainties which had bedevilled the Wesleys in earlier years.

As to the rest, we have already observed Charles Wesley's method of using scripture. The title line has the authority of Wisdom 11:25: 'But thou sparest all, for they are thine, O Lord, thou lover of souls.' From Psalm 51:1—'And under the shadow of thy wings shall be my refuge until this tyranny be overpast'—we get:

> Hide me, O my Saviour, hide
> Till the storm of life is past.

Even for his epithets Wesley had good scriptural authority: 'Just and holy is thy name' is based on Acts 3:14; 'Thou art full of truth and grace' on John 1:14. And that line in the last verse, 'Grace to cover all my sins', which some editors have altered, has the support of Psalm 85:2.

Nobody could accuse Wesley of being unscriptural. The crown of the hymn is in the last four lines. In Psalm 36:9 we read, 'For with thee is the fountain of life.' Wesley says, 'Thou of life the fountain art'. In Revelation 22:17 is the invitation, 'Whosoever will let him take the water of life freely.' Wesley continues, 'Freely let me take of thee'. And in John 4:14 Jesus says to the woman of Samaria, 'The water that I shall give him shall be in him a well of water springing up into everlasting life.' Wesley concludes:

> Spring thou up within my heart,
> Rise to all eternity.

Thus three passages, one from the Old Testament, one from Revelation and one from the Gospels, are welded together so spontaneously that the resultant quatrain amounts to a new creation.

Innumerable stories have been told of the use of this hymn as a prayer by people in peril. My favourite is about a singer entertaining tourists on an American river-boat in 1881. It being a Sunday evening, he ended his recital by singing two verses of 'Jesu, lover of my soul'. A stranger approached and asked him if he had fought in the Civil War. 'Yes', he replied, 'under General Grant.' 'I was on the other side,' said the stranger, 'and I think I heard you sing that hymn one bright night eighteen years ago. You were guarding a position we wanted to take. Being a sure shot, I was sent to pick you off. You were singing this hymn as you paced up and down. I had you in my sights and was about to fire when you came to the words "Cover my defenceless head With the shadow of thy wing." I couldn't fire after that.'

Rock of ages, cleft for me. Augustus Toplady (1740–78) was a zealous and dynamic preacher. Like the Wesley brothers, he had the comparatively rare experience of a 'new birth': it took place during his youth in Ireland, where he graduated at Trinity College, Dublin. In his short life he preached and wrote much; but he is remembered as the author of 'Rock of ages'. In the *Gospel Magazine* for October 1775, in an article signed Minimus, he wrote: 'Yet if you fall, be humbled; but do not despair. Pray afresh to God who is able to raise you up and set you on your feet again. Look to the blood of the covenant and say to the Lord from the depth of your heart,

> Rock of ages, cleft for me,
> Let me hide myself in thee:
> Foul, I to the fountain fly;
> Wash me, Saviour, or I die.'

Five months later in the same magazine, of which Toplady had become editor, the hymn appeared in full as we know it today—except that the author's line 'When my eyestrings break in death' was given its present form ('When my eyelids close') by Cotterill in 1815.

God is often called 'Rock' in the Old Testament. The title 'Rock of ages'—used also by Newton in 'Glorious things of thee are spoken'—is a literal translation of the Hebrew in Isaiah 26:4. In the New Testament this appellation and the qualities it suggests—shelter, stronghold, support—are transferred to Christ (1 Corinthians 10:4). Hence Toplady, remembering the 'cleft of the rock' which shielded Moses from the blinding glory of God's face, begins and ends his prayer. 'Rock of ages, cleft for me, Let me hide myself in thee.' In Christ we can stand before God without fear. Likewise, as the stricken rock at Meribah provided water in the drought, so from the pierced side of Christ on the cross came water and blood: water for cleansing, blood for atonement.

> Let the water and the blood,
> From thy riven side which flowed,
> Be of sin the double cure,
> Cleanse me from its guilt and power.

Sin is not only forgiven, it is expunged from the record. See Colossians 2:14 (NEB makes it clearer).

The rest of the hymn, a personal application of this belief, is summarised in a couplet which has been the dying prayer of many a Christian:

> Nothing in my hand I bring,
> Simply to thy cross I cling.

In this hymn we have the mystery of the atonement in a nutshell—or rather, in the cleft of a rock.

Abide with me. If there is one thing which humanity desires more than a refuge in trouble, it is a companion who can be trusted. Perhaps this is one of the reasons why the most popular hymn in the English-speaking world is Henry Lyte's 'Abide with me'. It expresses not only the desire for Christ's companionship but also the assurance of it.

The five verses generally sung today are undoubtedly the best of the original eight. Only one of the three now omitted, which stood between our second and third, would have added any appreciable new thought:

> Thou on my head in early youth didst smile;
> And, though rebellious and perverse meanwhile,
> Thou has not left me, oft as I left thee,
> On to the close, O Lord, abide with me.

This leads naturally to the familiar 'I need thy presence every passing hour'. There can be little doubt that Lyte intended the last stanza to balance the first, for there is an interesting parallelism in their subject-matter, after the manner of many of the psalms. The first line of each refers to the close of life; in the next line, 'darkness deepens' in the first verse is answered by 'shine through the gloom' in the last; likewise 'comforts flee' is matched by 'earth's vain shadows flee'; and the hymn ends with the three words with which it began.

The inclusion of 'Abide with me' among the evening hymns in Victorian hymnals caused some misunderstanding of its meaning. The exception is *Church Hymns* (1881). As John Ellerton, the editor, rightly points out: 'There is not throughout the hymn the slightest allusion to the close of the natural day ... It is far better adapted to be sung at funerals.' In fact it is of all general hymns the most general, since its subject is the continuous presence of Christ. If there is one season to which it is particularly suited, it is Easter, for the title is inspired by the Emmaus story, and the penultimate verse proclaims Hosea's challenging words, echoed by St Paul: 'O death, where is thy sting? O grave, where is thy victory?'

'Abide with me' is said to have been a favourite of King

George V and Queen Mary. In 1927 it was first sung at the FA Cup Final at Wembley on the suggestion of the Secretary, Sir Frederick Wall, who obtained the King's permission. (Cardiff beat Arsenal 1–0, the only time the cup has been won by a team outside England. The presence of so many Welshmen ensured the hymn a good send-off). A friend of mine who was present at the match in 1954 remembers a crowd of some 100,000 standing bareheaded to sing it.

Sun of my soul, thou Saviour dear. This hymn on the same Emmaus text, Luke 24:29, is a prayer within a poem entitled 'Evening' in Keble's *Christian Year.* The poem begins thus:

'Tis gone, that bright and orbed glaze,
Fast fading from our wistful gaze.
Yon mantling cloud has hid from sight
The last faint pulse of quivering light.

Only a countryman could fully appreciate this. After a further quatrain, which describes a traveller (170 years ago, remember) pressing on in the darkness, comes the first of the verses we know so well:

Sun of my soul, thou Saviour dear,
It is not night if thou be near:
O may no earth-born cloud arise
To hide thee from thy servant's eyes.

The reader will appreciate how perfectly the imagery here answers the statements in the poem's opening stanza. The beautiful metaphor, 'Sun of my soul', is, I think, unique.

Jesus, where'er thy people meet, and **Great Shepherd of thy people, hear:** kinship of subject often groups hymns in pairs. It is rare, however, for two much-used hymns on the same theme to have been written at the same time in the same village by two friends for the same occasion. I have already mentioned the *Olney Hymns* and the close association of their authors, John Newton, Rector of Olney, and William Cowper the poet. Many of these hymns were written for a weekly prayer meeting which Newton had inaugurated. It was so successful that the meeting-place was too small. The 'great room at the great house' was offered for the purpose.

Bull's life of Newton quotes him as saying in a letter, 'It is a noble place, with a parlour behind it, and holds a hundred and thirty people conveniently.' The two friends agreed that, for the first meeting in the great room, each should write a hymn. Cowper contributed 'Jesus, where'er thy people meet', and Newton a hymn beginning 'O Lord, our languid soul inspire', of which 'Dear Shepherd of thy people, hear'—now altered to 'Great Shepherd of thy people ...' is the second verse.

Editorial cuts in both hymns to fit them for ordinary church use have removed open allusions to the special circumstances of their composition; yet one who knows those circumstances will not miss the original intention of, for example, Cowper's petition:

> Dear Shepherd of thy chosen few,
> Thy former mercies here renew.

or of Newton's:

> As thou hast given a place for prayer
> So give us hearts to pray.

Inevitably associated by the date, place and purpose of their composition, these two hymns are contrasted in other respects. Newton's power lies in sincerity rather than style, whereas, as one expects, the touch of the professional poet gives distinction to Cowper's every line. Nor is the difference only literary. Each hymn throws a sidelight on its author's approach. Newton's prayer is based on human need; Cowper's rather upon Christ's ability to meet it. One can imagine the two friends praying aloud together:

Newton: Dear Shepherd of thy people, hear,
Thy presence now display.

Cowper: Where'er they seek thee thou art found,
And every place is hallowed ground.

Newton: Within these walls let holy peace
And love and concord dwell.

Cowper: For thou, within no walls confined,
Inhabitest the humble mind.

Newton: May we in faith receive thy word—

Cowper: Here to our waiting hearts proclaim
The sweetness of thy saving name.

Newton: —In faith present our prayers.

Cowper: Here we may prove the power of prayer
To strengthen faith and sweeten care,
To teach our faint desires to rise
And bring all heaven before our eyes.

That last line is a quotation from Milton's 'Il Penseroso'. After this the poet's thoughts rise far beyond the confines of 'the great room', where Newton is still left praying.

I need thee every hour. Annie Hawkes, an American, wrote these words in 1872 for Sunday School use. (The opening sentence recalls 'I need thy presence every passing hour' from 'Abide with me'). This little hymn still appears in *Mission Praise* and the latest Baptist and Methodist books. As an Anglican I might never have known it had not my maternal grandmother sung it to me when I was a child. Even today in the morning prayers the words spring spontaneously to my lips. Two recent authors have enlarged on the same theme: 'Jan Struther in 'Lord of all hopefulness' (A&M 394) and Brian Foley in 'Lord, as I wake I turn to you' (A&M 485).

O Christ of all the ages, come (HTC 262), by Michael Perry, also expresses the need for Christ's companionship, but less personally.

Christ in the stranger's guise (WS 13). The Emmaus story has inspired John Bell and his literary collaborator, Graham Maule, with the idea that Christ often meets us in the guise of a stranger met by chance and invited in for a meal. Other New Testament passages are brought to mind as the verses unfold, notably Matthew 25:34–40. In such encounters, the song remind us, we may be nearer to heaven on earth than we think.

One more step along the world I go (WS 64), sang Sydney Cater to his own straightforward tune in 1971. He looks at the world's changing values and lays them before Christ, his interpreter and guide. Nearly a quarter of a century on we still need to do the same—ideally after communion.

Shine, Jesus, shine! (WS 71) is one of Graham Kendrick's best-known songs. As we have already observed, he must be judged by what he says. John 12:46 is given as the basis of the song, but it is packed with scripture. The reader will find it a profitable exercise first to read in the Bible references and then to spot them in the stanza concerned. They are: in stanza 1, John 1:5, 8:12, 8:32; in stanza 2, Hebrews 9:14, 15 and Psalm 139:23; in stanza 3, Exodus 34:29, 30 and 2 Corinthians 3:18; and in stanza 4, Hebrews 1:3, Acts 2:3, 4, Isaiah 66:12, and Genesis. 1:3.

Make me a channel of your peace. Sebastian Temple, a Roman Catholic, has earned the gratitude of all Christians for making this Franciscan prayer singable.

PRAYER TO GOD THE HOLY SPIRIT has been plentifully voiced in hymns, yet all too few of them do justice to the subject's true scope and limitless potential. In Julian's Dictionary (second edition) over 200 such hymns are catalogued, and three-quarters of them begin with the word 'Come'. Many are translations of either the ninth-century *Veni Creator* or the thirteenth-century Golden Sequence, *Veni, sancte Spiritus*. The authorship of both these ancient hymns is unknown, and neither of them has been done full justice in translation.

Veni Creator. The translation by Robert Bridges—A&M (1950) 152, EH (1906) 154—is the nearest English approach to the sturdy ninth-century Latin. But it is never likely to replace Bishop Cosin's 'Come, Holy Ghost' in popular affection; indeed attempts to do this on national occasions have failed. Through its inclusion in the 1662 Prayer Book, Cosin's version came to be regarded almost as holy writ. This is a pity. In the first place it is not a true translation but rather a condensed paraphrase. It is surprising and regrettable that Cosin ignored the Latin word *Creator:* surprising since it is one of the two words by which the hymn is generally known; regrettable because creative activity is one of the Spirit's scriptural attributes. Again, Cosin makes use of words like 'unction' and 'comfort' which no longer mean what they did in his day and are therefore misleading to modern ears.

Cosin wrote 'Come, Holy Ghost' for private use as early as 1627, against the background of the Thirty Years' War on the Continent and the mounting Puritan pressure at home which was to culminate in the Civil War. 'Keep far our foes, give peace *at home*', a heartfelt prayer, seems to have been prompted as much by current unrest as by the Latin, which says nothing about peace *at home*.

Very different is the scene reflected in John Dryden's stately paraphrase, written in the last decade of the same century: **Creator Spirit, by whose aid.** By then the years of religious persecution were over. Although he turned Roman Catholic on the accession of James II and refused to sign the oath of allegiance to William III, Dryden seems, apart from being deprived of his laureateship, to have lived the rest of his life in comfort. This paraphrase, in which the terse Latin lines are gracefully embellished, certainly speaks of more settled and complacent times. No mention here of foes, ghostly or otherwise. The emphasis is on social improvement rather than survival. And note that the Latin word *Creator* in the first line, ignored by Cosin, is here given the prominence that befits the age of Sir Isaac Newton.

Both the scientific advances and consequent sophistication of Dryden's day, and the political and religious turbulence of Cosin's, have their counterparts in the twentieth century. Both versions of *Veni Creator* are relevant today.

Veni sancte Spiritus. The best English version is that of J. M. Neale (1854): 'Come, thou Holy Paraclete'. It gains strength as well as distinction through having preserved the original Latin metre. It is still a mystery to me why the revisers of A&M preferred to cling to the commonplace version, 'Come, thou Holy Spirit, come', based on Caswall, when Neale's was ready to hand—see EH (1906). Not only is Neale nearer to the Latin, both in metre and meaning, but his language is more finely focused. For example, take the third and sixth lines of the first verse. Where Neale has 'Send thy light and brilliancy', A&M has 'Shed a ray of light divine'; Where Neale has 'Come, the soul's true radiancy', A&M has 'Come, within our bosoms shine'.

Come down, O love divine. How fortunate we are in this stirring translation by R.F. Littledale from the Italian of the fourteenth-century monk, Bianco da Siena! Its unique metre and the stately tune written for it by Vaughan Williams each contribute to its distinction. It is also outstanding as being the earliest hymn to develop St Paul's claim that first among the gifts of the Spirit is love, the greatest power in the world and the root of all goodness. The first line is a refreshing form of address to the third person of the Trinity.

O Holy Spirit, Lord of grace. This is a translation by John Chandler of a comparatively modern prayer-hymn to the Holy Spirit for the gift of mutual love: *O fons amoris Spiritus*. It is by the French scholar Charles Coffin, Rector of the University of Paris, who in 1736 was commissioned by his Archbishop to make the third revision of the Parisian Breviary. (It had already been revised in 1527 and 1680.) Coffin contributed 83 hymns of his own, this one replacing the ancient office hymn for Terce (see EH 255). Chandler's translation was included in his *Hymns of the Primitive Church* (1837). From his preface it is clear that he thought the hymns in the Parisian Breviary were ancient; most of them were then little more than a century old.

Gracious Spirit, Holy Ghost. Bishop Christopher Wordsworth's paraphrase of the BCP Epistle for Quinquagesima appeared in his *Holy Year* (1862). No versification of this passage could possibly match the peerless prose of the Authorized Version, and some of the original eight stanzas are now omitted. The five or six generally sung, being in prayer form, meet the need of a hymnic response to the reading of 1 Corinthians 13.

Gracious Spirit, dwell with me. In 1855 a Congregational minister, Thomas Toke Lynch, published a collection of hymns entitled *The Rivulet*, for the use of his own congregation. This is one of his best contributions. It is a simple prayer for the fulfilment of the promise in John 14:17: 'He dwelleth with you and shall be in you.' Two of the six stanzas, those beginning 'Tender Spirit' and 'Silent Spirit', are often omitted. Lynch's hymns, like his sermons, had a freshness and sparkle which contrasted strikingly with the dour, doctinaire religion of other Dissenters of his day.

Holy Spirit, truth divine. This is another hymn which editors of Anglican hymnals seem to have regarded with suspicion. It was banished from A&M in 1950. The author was Samuel Longfellow, the American Unitarian minister.

This is a prayer for fruits of the Spirit: four (love, joy, peace and goodness) from St Paul's list and two (truth and power) promised by our Lord. The last line, 'Spring, O well, for ever spring' is from Numbers 21:17.

Breathe on me, breath of God. A fresh title for the Holy Spirit! This fine little hymn of 1878 by the Oxford scholar Edwin Hatch glows with the same fire as 'Come down, O love divine'. Both hymns go far beyond the usual petitions for comfort, guidance, influence and grace. Here the Holy Spirit is entreated to convert and fill the life of the singer. The hymn has been robbed of much of its strength through association with unsuitable tunes (see chapter 8).

Eternal ruler of the ceaseless round. J.W. Chadwick, a young American Unitarian, wrote this 'song of peace and goodwill' in 1864, during the Civil War. This noble hymn, addressed to the Holy Spirit throughout, was introduced to this country by Garrett Horder in *Congregational Hymns* (1884), and to Anglicans by Percy Dearmer in EH (1906).

O King, enthroned on high: A faithful translation by J. Brownlie of an eighth-century fragment from the Greek office for Pentecost—though 'comforter' does not convey the true meaning of 'Paraklete'. The title 'King' strikes a new chord: at least the Holy Spirit is seen as a majestic and attractive person.

Spirit divine, attend our prayers. The author, Andrew Reed, a Congregationalist, is better known as the founder of homes for orphaned and handicapped children than for his writings. This hymn first appeared in the **Evangelical Magazine** for June 1829. It is a prayer to the Holy Spirit based on the various symbols of his activity: light to guide, fire to purge, dew to regenerate, dove to bring peace, wind to invigorate. All except the dew, which may allude to Hosea 14:5, are from the New Testament. These words need a dynamic tune: Nativity fits them well.

O Holy Ghost, they people bless. Sir Henry Baker wrote this hymn on Tuesday in Whitsun-week 1873 and printed it in his parish magazine at Monkland. The tune, St Timothy, is also his. A welcome breeze blows through both words and music. In verse 2 the worshipper is led to open his life to the Holy Spirit's influence; verse 3 alludes to the creation

(Genesis 1:2), verse 4 to Pentecost. The fifth verse, recalling Song of Solomon 4:16, and the sixth, add little to the substance of the first four.

Spirit of mercy, truth and love. The authorship of this useful little eighteenth-century hymn is unknown. The theme of its petition is in the second couplet:

And still from age to age convey
The wonders of this sacred day.

There is strong scriptural support for the belief that the charismatic manifestations of Pentecost are still available to the Church wherever there is sufficient faith. This was assumed by Charles Wesley when he wrote:

Lord, we believe to us and ours
 The apostolic promise given:
We wait the pentecostal powers
 The Holy Ghost sent down from heaven.

In his next stanza he cites Acts 2:39 as his authority. Few other hymnists have expressed this faith. James Montgomery did so in 'Lord God the Holy Ghost', and Albert Midlane in his missionary hymns 'O Spirit of the living God' and 'Revive thy work, O God'. But they are less widely sung nowadays. It is good, however, to see twentieth-century writers filling the gap.

O breath of life, come sweeping through us. Bessie Porter Head wrote this hymn over sixty years ago, and it still has a timely message for the Church today. The tune Commandments would carry these words well.

Filled with the Spirit's power, by J.R. Peacey, cries out to the Holy Spirit for gifts of fellowship, unity and love. Cyril Taylor's comments on it in *Hymns for Today Discussed* are helpful.

Holy Spirit come, confirm us. This short but comprehensive prayer by Fr Brian Foley appeared in the *New Catholic Hymnal* (1971). It now fills a gap in Methodist, URC, Baptist and Anglican worship.

Fire of God (HTC 234). Having already called for more hymns to do justice to the Holy Spirit's limitless power, I ought to welcome this hymn by Michael Saward. 'Fire of

God', 'Wind of God', 'Voice of God', 'dynamic', 'prophetic'—these are apt and powerful epithets. But I cannot help feeling that 'titanic' in this context is unfortunate, on three counts: it usually connotes material bulk; Titan was a heathen god; and the name *Titanic* is associated with one of the most tragic disasters in our maritime history. 'Stupendous', perhaps.

Let every Christian pray, with the refrain 'Come, Holy Spirit, come', is the work of Fred Pratt Green, the foremost Methodist hymn-writer of this century. In the intervening lines he reminds us that the Church, since her birth at Pentecost, has been inhabited by the Holy Spirit. The gifts of the Spirit have never been withdrawn from those who ask in faith.

Nearly half the contents of any standard collection are hymns addressed to God about ourselves. Those discused in this chapter are but a few of the best known. From the days of the Hebrew Psalter, hymns have been used for corporate prayer; and it is still true that when John and Jane Citizen face a crisis and want to pray they will be more likely to remember the words of a hymn than anything else.

5 HYMNS TO US ABOUT GOD: TEACHING

THE CUSTOM OF SINGING TO EACH OTHER about God and our faith dates back to the early Christian hymn-writers and beyond them to the Hebrew Psalter. Psalm 29, for example, is all addressed to the worshipper about God's creative power and providence. Many Christian hymns of all ages take this form; it is of course an oblique way of praising God, but the main object is to deepen faith and reverence—in other words to teach. Nearly all sacred songs contain some teaching; those addressed to God in praise and prayer have much to tell us about the object of our worship, as we have already seen. In this chapter our concern is with hymns written with the prime purpose of teaching: hymns addressed to us about God.

Firmly I believe and truly. John Henry Newman's poem *The dream of Gerontius* was published in 1866, but these lines were not extracted for use in public worship until the publication of EH forty years later. Since then the hymn has appeared in WH (1939), A&M, *Church Hymnary* (third edition, 1973), WOV (1975) and, altered, in HTC (1982). These dying words of Gerontius are an affirmation of his simple faith in the Holy Trinity, the manhood and saving power of God the Son, the Holy Ghost—'Him the holy, him the strong'—and the Church as guardian of the truth. It is the Creed in a nutshell. We shall see presently that every article of the Apostles' Creed is illuminated in the hymn book.

I bind unto myself today. The legend of St Patrick's Breastplate, as this hymn is called, has been told by others. The earliest known Irish text has been dated some 300 years after St Patrick's time. It is not impossible, however, that the rugged saint sang something similar in his encounter with the Druids. We must be grateful to R.A.S. Macalister and James Quinn for their more literal and concise translations: 'Today I arise', and 'This day God gives me', respectively. But they have not the appeal of Mrs Alexander's pictorial style, nor of the fine Irish melody which she must have had in mind. Her eighth stanza, 'Christ be with me', is often used as a separate hymn.

In this chapter I group a number of hymns under each of the Creed's statements.

I BELIEVE IN GOD THE FATHER ALMIGHTY. It is the business of a poet to express common experience in quotable phrase. In this respect William Cowper (1731–1800) is outstanding among English poets of the first rank who have turned their hand to hymn-writing. Of his sixty-eight hymns, **God moves in a mysterious way** is, I believe, the last he wrote; it is also his greatest. The first line has reached proverbial status. The second half of the first verse is founded on Psalm 77:19 and Psalm 104:3; and the sixth verse is an exposition of John 13:7. But the hymn is loaded with original gems, for example:

> Behind a frowning providence
> He hides a smiling face.

and

> The bud may have a bitter taste
> But sweet will be the flower.

These two couplets have a familiar ring to Englishmen, whether they go to church or not. The hymn was headed 'Light shining out of darkness', and it deals with a common experience: the dark patches in life when faith wavers. Few suffered more from them than Cowper. So there is both sincerity and authority in his advice:

> Ye fearful saints, fresh courage take;
> The clouds ye so much dread
> Are big with mercy, and shall break
> In blessings on your head.

Can man, by searching, find out God? (A&M 438). Here a living author, Elizabeth Cosnett, throws light on an old problem. On the authority of Hebrews 1:1–3 she directs us to Christ, the brightness of God and 'the very image of his person'. In stanza 3 she sets earthly values 'beside the manger and the cross'. Thus in stanza 4 we are moved to penitence, 'the starting-point for praise'.

MAKER OF HEAVEN AND EARTH.

That elegant piece of poetry based on Psalm 19:1–6, **The spacious firmament on high**, speaks for itself. Its author, Joseph Addison, published it in the *Spectator*, a daily paper which he ran for nearly two years in collaboration with Richard Steel 'to enlighten morality with wit and to temper wit with morality'. In this paper Addison's three best-known hymns appeared in 1712: 'The Lord my pasture shall prepare on 26 July; 'When all thy mercies, O my God' on 9 August; and 'The spacious firmament on high' on 23 August. On 19 August there appeared a letter from Isaac Watts, saying that the hymns in the *Spectator* had moved him to try his hand at versifying the Psalms. He appended his first attempt, on Psalm 114. His *Psalms of David* were completed seven years later.

John Sheeles, a contemporary musician, wrote the tune named Addison's for 'The spacious firmament'. It suits the words well. So does Tallis's Canon, as Britten has shown in *Noye's Fludde.*

Our next author has taught more people the fundamentals of Christian faith than many sermons. Cecil Frances Humphreys (later the wife of William Alexander, who became an Irish bishop) was teaching her young godchildren the church Catechism, and although they could repeat the Apostles' Creed by heart, she knew they did not understand it. The young godmother thereupon wrote a series of simple verses to explain the Creed and other parts of the Cathechism. The result was a volume entitled *Hymns for Little Children*, published in 1848; it ran to 100 editions.

All things bright and beautiful. Educationists now claim that not until the age of 13-plus are children ready for abstract thinking. Mrs Alexander anticipated them by 140 years and more. In this hymn on the first credal statement, 'I believe in God the Father almighty, maker of heaven and earth', she paints a colourful picture of nature. It has been fashionable in recent years to omit the stanza:

The rich man in his castle,
 The poor man at his gate,

God made them, high or lowly,
And ordered their estate.

Social differences, it is claimed, are man-made. This is only partly true. What control, for example, has the human race over such things as personality, physical features, intelligence, natural skills and other characteristics which determine our fortune in life? The emphasis of this verse is certainly out of line with the rest of the hymn, which is about the beauties of nature; but its clear allusion to our Lord's parable of the rich man and Lazarus may have something to teach us about Christian stewardship.

AND IN JESUS CHRIST HIS ONLY SON OUR LORD, WHO WAS CONCEIVED BY THE HOLY GHOST, BORN OF THE VIRGIN MARY ... This means nothing to a child. Yet there must be millions of people who have formed their earliest picture of the birth of Jesus Christ from the story Mrs Alexander tells in **Once in royal David's city**. Reading it through, one can imagine the author's telling the story to an enthralled group of children. For simplicity of language and directness of thought this hymn must be without equal. Of its 218 words, only 46 have more than one syllable and only 'obedient' and 'redeeming' more than two. No alterations have been made to the text and the hymn is generally sung in its entirely. The only verse occasionally omitted is that beginning 'And through all his wondrous childhood', in which the author breaks off for a couple of lines to moralise about the conduct expected of Christian children.

All Christmas and Epiphany hymns contain teaching. They fall into two categories: narrative—like the one we have just discussed—and doctrinal.

The narrative hymns need little introduction. '**While shepherds watched**' is a verse paraphrase of Luke 2:8–14 by Nahum Tate of Tate and Brady. '**Behold the great Creator makes Himself a house of clay**' is from a lovely poem, 'Fairest of morning lights appear', by Thomas Pestel, chaplain to Charles I. James Montgomery's '**Angels from the realms of glory**', by inviting angels, shepherds, sages and saints to join us in adoration of the Christ-child, brings the

Christmas story into the context of modern worship. **'Christians awake'** was written by John Byrom, a colourful Manchester character, as a Christmas present for his daughter, Dorothy. His MS has 48 lines. As no more than 36 have appeared in any one hymn book and alterations have been made, the reader may be interested to see the original, a facsimile of which is here produced by kind permission of the Chetham Library, Manchester.

The Doctrinal hymns propound in various ways the teaching of the season. First **O come, all ye faithful.** The Latin hymn *Adeste fideles*, in four stanzas, with its fine tune, are believed to have been written by J.F. Wade in France in about 1743. The first English translation in the same metre, beginning 'Ye faithful, approach ye', was made by Frederick Oakley in 1841 and sung at Margaret Chapel in London (now All Saints', Margaret Street) where Oakley was incumbent; but it remained unpublished until 1852, when it appeared as 'O come, all ye faithful' in Murray's Hymnal. The middle stanzas (3, 4 and 5), also in Latin but added later, were translated by W.T. Brooke in 1884.

It is not easy to do Latin verse into English and preserve both metre and meaning. Stanza 2 presents a problem:

> *Deum de Deo,*
> *Lumen de lumine,*
> *Gestant puellae viscera.*

Oakley's first two lines,

> God of God,
> Light of light,

like the Latin, are majestic in their terseness. The metrical irregularity is deliberate and the tune easily adjusted. The third line, however, Oakley evades, falling back on words from the *Te Deum*: 'Thou didst not abhor the Virgin's womb' is a fair sixteenth-century rendering of *non horruisti virginis uterum*, but not of this line. In any case the modern connotation of the word 'abhor' is unacceptable in this context; it is therefore regrettable that it has been perpetuated. Either John Ellerton's translation of this line in *Church Hymns* (1871), 'Comes to the world as a maiden's child', or the one

Christmas Day for Dolly

Christians awake, salute the happy Morn
Whereon the Saviour of the World was born
Rise to adore the Mystery of Love
Which Hosts of Angels chanted from above
With them the joyfull Tidings first begun
Of God incarnate & the Virgins Son
Then to the watchfull Shepherds it was told
Who heard th' Angelic Heralds Voice—behold!
~~To you and~~
I bring good Tidings of the Saviours Birth
To you and all the Nations upon Earth
This day hath God fullfill'd his promis'd Word
This day is born a Saviour Xt the Lord
In David city Shepherds ye shall find
The long foretold redeemer of Mankind
Wrapt up in swadling Cloaths, be this the Sign
A Cratch contains the holy Babe divine
He spake, & straightway the celestial Quire
In Hymns of Joy unknown before conspire
The Praises of redeeming Love they sung
And Heav'ns whole Orb with Hallelujahs rung
God Highest Glory was their Anthem still
Peace upon Earth & mutual Good Will

The Christmas Hymn written by John Byrom (1692–1763) for his daughter Dorothy. From the original in Chethams Library, Manchester, by kind permission.

To Bethlehem straight th' enlightned Shepherds ran
To see the Wonder God had wrought for Man
They saw their Saviour as the Angel said
The swaddled Infant in the Manger laid
Joseph & Mary a distressed Pair
Guard the sole Object of th' almighty's Care
To human Eyes none present but they two
Where Heaven was pointing its concentred View
Amaz'd the wonorous Story they proclaim
Th' [illegible] ~~Fame~~
The first Apostles of his Infant Fame
But Mary kept & ponderd in her Heart
The heavnly Vision wch the Swains impart
They to their Flocks & praising God return
With Hearts no doubt yt did within them burn
Let us like these good Shepherds then employ
Our gratefull Voices to proclaim the Joy
Like Mary let us ponder in our Mind
Gods wondrous Love in saving lost Mankind
Artless & watchfull as these favour'd Swains
While Virgin Meekness in the Heart remains
Trace we the Babe who has retriev'd our Loss
From his poor Manger to his bitter Cross
Follow we him who has our Cause maintain'd
And Man's first heavnly State shall be regain'd

Then may we hope th' Angelic Thrones among
To sing, redeem'd, a glad triumphal Song
He that was born upon this joyfull Day
Around us all his Glory shall display
Sav'd by his Love incessant we shall sing
Of Angels, & of Angel-Men the King

in the *New Catholic Hymnal* (1971), 'Born of a maiden in humility', conveys the true meaning of this line. The first two lines of the stanza are best left as Oakley wrote them.

Of the Father's heart begotten. The original Latin, *Corde natus ex parentis*, is part of a poem by the fourth-century Spanish poet Aurelius Prudentius. After a successful legal career, he retired at the age of 57 to a monastery, where he wrote several books of sacred poetry, including the *Cathemerinon* (the daily round), from which these verses are taken. The refrain *saeculorum saeculis*—evermore and evermore—was added in the Middle Ages, when the cento was made for use as a Christmas hymn. In its present form it is a fine expression of the divinity of Christ, echoing the prologue to the fourth Gospel and passages from the book of Revelation.

A great and mighty wonder. This translation by J.M. Neale of a seventh-century Greek hymn is on the same theme. Neal wrote it in six four-line verses, his third being:

And we with them triumphant
Repeat the hymn again:
To God on high be glory,
And peace on earth to men!

It was a happy thought of Dearmer's to omit the first line of this verse and use the other three as a refrain, thus matching these words with the old German carol melody which has made them popular.

Hark! the herald angels sing. Charles Wesley's *Hymns and Sacred Poems* (1739) contained three great seasonal hymns. The one for Christmas began 'Hark! how all the welkin rings'. Our three ten-line verses, beginning 'Hark! the herald angels sing' (A&M 35), are pure Wesley except lines, 1,2,7 and 8 of verse 1, two words in verse 2, and the refrain. Mendelssohn's tune—a male-chorus from his secular cantata *Festgesang*—was first set to these words in 1855 by W.H. Cummings, organist of Waltham Abbey. In 1857 it appeared in Chope's *Congregational Hymn and Tune Book*, and in 1861 in A&M. Mendelssohn (who died in 1847) was pleased with the tune but thought it unsuited to sacred words. Nevertheless Cummings's judgement was right. The melody, indissolubly married to this hymn, which is a glorious exposition of the scheme of our salvation, has carried its message to Christians and non-Christians all over the world.

In the bleak mid-winter. Here Christina Rossetti has given us a poetic meditation on the birth of Jesus. It is a fine example of the use of poetry to express feeling. Even its metrical irregularities have a purpose. Note, for example, the cumulative effect of the crowded line, 'Snow had fallen, snow on snow', as against the repetition of 'Snow on snow', isolated in the next-line to depict the bareness of the scene. Note also the moving use of antithesis in verses 2,3 and 4, contrasting the heavenly glory of the Son of God with the inhospitable world he came to save. On reaching verse 5 one is ready for self-dedication.

Two American hymns deserve mention. One is **O little town of Bethlehem,** a meditation on the human blessings of Christmas, written by Phillips Brooks in 1868 before he became a bishop. He was noted as a preacher and for his ministry to children. This hymn was written for his Sunday school. EH includes his beautiful fourth verse:

> Where children pure and happy
>   Pray to the blessed child,
> Where misery cries out to thee,
>   Son of the mother mild;
> Where charity stands watching
>   And faith holds wide the door,
> The dark night wakes, the glory breaks,
>   And Christmas comes once more.

The other, **It came upon the midnight clear**, by Edmund Sears, a Unitarian minister who believed in and preached the divinity of Christ, stresses the social messages of Christmas.

Brightest and best, one of Heber's loveliest hymns, was at first suspect because it was thought to be addressed to a star. But the first line surely refers to Revelation 22:16, where 'the bright and morning star' is Jesus himself, the ultimate fulfiller of the prophecy of Balaam in Numbers 24:17. He is *der Morgenstern* of the glorious German hymn, 'How brightly shines the morning star' (New EH 27, AH 130), by Philipp Nicolai. In Heber's hymn, then, we pray to Christ, 'the bright and morning star' to come to our aid, and then in the third line we ask for a 'star of the East' to lead us to worship him as it did the Wise Men—a star to lead us to the star.

The people that in darkness sat is a paraphrase of Isaiah 9:1–7 based on the one in Morrison's *Scottish Paraphrases*, of which NEH 57 is the original form, omitting the verse about Midian. The version in A&M is closer to the AV text. The omission of verses 3 and 7 makes the hymn more compact. The best tune for these words is St Magnus, partly because it fits them perfectly and partly by reason of its association with Ascensiontide.

Glory to God! All heaven with joy is ringing (A&M 462). Canon John E. Bowers, while Vicar of Ashby de la Zouch, wrote this noble hymn with Sir Richard Runciman Terry's equally noble tune in mind. It links, as no other hymn does, the coming of Christ in the past at Bethlehem with his coming in the present at the Eucharist.

SUFFERED UNDER PONTIUS PILATE, WAS CRUCIFIED, DEAD AND BURIED ... Mrs Alexander's third credal hymn, **There is a green hill far away**, is founded on this clause. One might have expected another narrative hymn, telling the story of the Passion; there is plenty of material in the Gospels. But the wise godmother has avoided that and concerns herself with the purpose of it all.

The first verse is a colourful statement of our Lord's crucifixion and death. The 'green hill' is pure poetic licence. The Gospels simply say 'the place called the Skull' (Aramaic *Golgotha*, Latin *Calvaria*). It may have been a low rounded hill shaped like a skull, but there is no evidence that it was green; rather the contrary. The green hill to which Mrs Alexander alludes is outside the city of Derry. She knew it well and so did her godchildren. Being a good teacher, she used a familiar sight as a starting-point. There can be no doubt that this picture has contributed to the hymn's popularity. The second line is less felicitious. It was pointed out to Mrs Alexander that the archaism '*Without* a city wall' would be misunderstood (as it certainly has been), and she reluctantly permitted it to be altered to '*Outside* a city wall', which is ugly. *Beyond* would have been better.

The statement in the first verse prompts four questions, to which the four succeeding verses provide the answers. Why did Jesus suffer? 'We believe it was for us.' Why was it necessary? 'He died that we might be forgiven.' Why did it have to be Jesus? 'There was no other good enough.' How can we thank him? 'O dearly, dearly has he loved, And we must love him too, And trust in his redeeming blood, And try his works to do.' These are questions often asked about the atonement. And how easy it is to get out of one's depth in trying to answer them—particularly to children! The popularity of this hymn is evidence that a simple answer is all that most people need.

The cross, symbol of our faith, has been regarded in a variety of ways by Christian hymn-writers. The sign of the cross as an outward profession of Christian faith dates back to the apostles. Early precedent for its use to banish temptation is found in the fourth-century poem *Ades Pater supreme*, by Prudentius, a cento of which is given in NEH 80: see verses 2, 3 and 6.

To the sixth-century poet Venantius Fortunatus the cross was a tree of glory from which Christ reigned, and also a trick whereby the Devil was deceived: see *Vexilla regis* (A&M 58, NEH 79, verses 3–5). David's prophecy refers to Psalm 96:10. The words 'from the tree' were added to this text in a Christian gloss found in Justin, Tertullian and others.

In the Middle Ages the emphasis shifted to Christ's suffering: the majesty gave place to the crucifix. This is reflected in the thirteenth-century poem *Salve caput cruentatum*, on which Paul Gerhardt based the hymn known in England as 'O sacred head, sore wounded'.

Since the seventeenth century there has been a return to glorying in the cross as an expression of God's love. The implications of Galatians 2:20 are set forth in Samuel Crossman's moving poem, 'My song is love unknown'. The same theme is spelt out for children by Walsham How in 'It is a thing most wonderful'. To Toplady, author of 'Rock of ages', the cross is the payment of a debt, as we saw in chapter 4.

Praise to the Holiest in the height. Like 'Firmly I believe and truly', this is an abstract from Newman's *Dream of Gerontius*. It is the song of a choir of angelicals, overheard by the soul as it nears the divine presence. Three years after the completion of the poem these verses were included in the Appendix to A&M with the tune *Gerontius*, specially composed by Dykes. Here is expressed, as in no other hymn, the relationship between the fall of the first Adam in the garden of Eden (Genesis 3) and the victory of the second Adam over the same temptation in the wilderness (Matthew 4). The parallelism of these two passages is so striking that it might reasonably be assumed that the New Testament story, like the Old, is allegorical. Be that as it may, the truth still remains as summed up in Newman's second stanza:

> O loving wisdom of our God!
> When all was sin and shame,
> A second Adam to the fight
> And to the rescue came.

Or, as St Paul puts it: 'As by one man's disobedience many were made sinners, so by one man's obedience many will be made righteous' (Romans 5:19). Herein is that 'wisest love' proclaimed in verse 3. These verses are so supremely singable that it is fatally easy to roll them off the tongue without taking in their meaning. The fourth verse is perhaps the least understood. It means, I think, that human nature had become so corrupt that grace alone could not make a man sinless: the 'higher gift' of God's own presence in flesh and blood was needful, to ensure the offering of one perfect human life. Verses 5 and 6 return to the manhood of Christ. 'The double agony in man'—the burden of guilt and the prospect of death—was endured by Christ in the garden and on the cross on man's behalf. What love could be more generous than that?

Recent twentieth-century writers see man's inhumanity to man as involving us all in the crucifixion. Tim Ree's 'O crucified Redeemer' (A&M 404), Erik Routley's deeply moving 'There in God's garden' (A&M 514), and Graham Kendrick's 'Come and see' are examples. Also significant is the growing popularity of the spiritual 'Were you there?' At a three-hour devotion one Good Friday in the Sixties I asked a talented young bass from my choir to sing it after one of my addresses. It was then regarded as an innovation. It is now in all the hymn books.

Morning glory, starlit sky (A&M 496, WS 56). Canon W.H. Vanstone, one of our foremost living theologians, refused preferments and university appointments to stay on the Rochdale housing estate of which he was the first vicar. After some thirty years there, overwork began to undermine his health. He then accepted a residentiary canonry at Chester Cathedral, where he devoted himself to preaching and writing. His first book, *Love's Endeavour, Love's Expense*, published in 1977, threw fresh light on the nature of God. All thinking people should read it. On its last page is this hymn. Here the author sees in the cross what God's love for his creation has cost him. Originally it had seven verses all addressed to God. The editors of A&M, with the author's co-operation, have omitted his second verse and addressed the hymn to the worshippers: harmless and helpful emendations. In their version verse 4 recalls 2 Corinthians 6–10; verse 5 has the authority of John 14:9. The tune composed for WS by Barry Rose is ideal for the words, easy to learn and rewarding.

Each of these hymns shows us the cross from a different aspect; none by itself gives the whole picture. We need them all to bring us to the frame of mind in which Isaac Watts penned the greatest passion hymn of all time, 'When I survey the wondrous cross'. Read it now. It is in every standard hymn book; it is also in *The Penguin Book of Hymns* with the original text and a helpful introduction by Ian Bradley.

HE DESCENDED INTO HELL. Much confusion has been caused by the use of the English word 'hell' to denote both the place of torment and the abode of the departed awaiting resurrection; as also of 'paradise' to mean the latter as well as heaven. The 'hell' of the Creed is the 'paradise' of Luke 24:43, where Christ promised to be with the penitent thief, and to which Peter referred in his first sermon (Acts 2:27) and in his Epistle (1 Peter 3:19 and 4:6).

It is finished! Blessed Jesus. For the 1875 edition of A&M, Archbishop Maclagan wrote this hymn for Easter Even, dwelling not, as others had done, on the sepulchre, grave-clothes and grief-stricken disciples, but rather on where Jesus was and what we believe he was doing between his death and his resurrection. As rewritten and greatly improved by the author in 1902, it remains the only hymn on this credal statement in use today.

THE THIRD DAY HE ROSE AGAIN. All Easter hymns proclaim the gospel of the resurrection, but none so briefly and simply as **Jesus Christ is risen today.** It is as much part of the plain man's Easter as is 'Hark! The herald' of his Christmas. Both were added to the *Supplement to the New Version* of the Psalms early in the nineteenth century; both had been altered a good deal over the years. Nobody knows who wrote either the Easter hymn, 'Jesus Christ is risen today', or the old Latin carol on which it is based, '*Surrexit Christus hodie*'. Amid festive alleluias it states the fact of our Lord's resurrection and man's salvation through the cross.

For poetic fire and scriptural content this hymn offers nothing to compare with Charles Wesley's Easter Day hymn, 'Christ the Lord is risen today', sung by Methodists with alleluias, to the same tune as the above and therefore liable to be confused with it. Originally it had eleven stanzas and, not surprisingly, never seems to have been sung in its entirety. Percy Dearmer, however, without altering a word, presented it in EH in a way that solved three problems: omitting Wesley's first stanza, he gave the hymn a distinctive first line; omitting the alleluias, he dissociated it from the tune of 'Jesus Christ is risen today'; and selecting the five stanzas 2, 3, 4, 5 and 10, he provided the compact and valuable hymn which follows.

Love's redeeming work is done. These five stirring stanzas embody the quintessence of Charles Wesley's art. Take the line, 'Lo! Our sun's eclipse is o'er'—a metaphor suggested by Malachi 4:2 and the three hours' darkness at the crucifixion. In six short words the death of Christ is seen as a shadow that passes, leaving his splendour undiminished. Note, too, the economy of the line 'Vain the stone, the watch, the seal', and compare Matthew 27:66. The next line substantiates Matthew 6:18, 'The gates of hell shall not prevail ...'; and the third echoes Romans 6:9, 'Death has no more dominion over him.' 'Paradise' in the fourth line is the opposite of hell, and therefore in this context means heaven. The third stanza is a shout of triumph. Like the fifth, it should be sung in unison. The rhetorical force of St Paul's exclamation, 'O Death, where is thy sting? O grave, where is thy victory?' is heightened by the rhyming statement with which Wesley precedes each taunting question:

> Lives again our glorious King;
> Where, O death, is now thy sting?
> Dying once, he all doth save;
> Where they victory, O grave?

After this, our feet leave the ground. 'Made like him' (1 John 3:2): human nature is restored to the exalted position for which it was created. The last verse of this selection is addressed to Christ. It is Wesley's tenth; his eleventh is given in the *Methodist Hymn Book*. It will be noted that in each of these five verses our Lord is given a different name: Sun, Christ, King, Head, Resurrection. Set to the tuneful German melody Savannah, culled by Vaughan Williams from a collection compiled by John Wesley for use in his 'Foundery' chapel in 1742, 'Love's redeeming work is done' has passed from EH to other collections, including A&M (1950), and is now one of the most-sung Easter hymns.

O sons and daughters. The original Latin is by Jean Tisserand, a fifteenth-century Parisian friar. It is entirely narrative; its allusions to Thomas make it particularly appropriate to Low Sunday (Easter 1). A simpler and purer form of the melody, arranged by Walford Davies, is in NEH.

The reader will remember from chapter 1 the eighth-century Greek canons—long hymns of praise and teaching for various seasons. In Athens to this day towards midnight on Easter Even a crowd gathers at the church, usually in the square outside, and waits in darkness and silence holding unlighted tapers. On the stroke of twelve a gun is fired. The priest elevates the cross and exclaims 'Christ is risen.' The crowd shouts back the greeting; tapers are lighted from hand to hand, spreading beams of light in all directions; drums and trumpets sound, and the Easter canon is sung.

The Canon for Easter day is the work of St John of Damascus, the most distinguished writer in this genre. It consists of eight odes of which Neale made English metrical centos in *Hymns of the Eastern Church* (1862). 'The day of resurrection' is the first ode; 'Thou hallowed chosen morn of praise' the eighth.

Come ye faithful, raise the strain is the first ode of the Canon for Low Sunday by the same author. Compare Neale's fine translation of verse 4 in EH with the contrived doxology in A&M, which was planted in the appendix to the first edition of that influential book in 1868 and has regrettably taken root. It is an instance of a pernicious Victorian custom which we shall discuss at the end of Chapter 6.

The association of Christ's resurrection with Israel's deliverance from Egypt, appropriate when the gospel was addressed to Jews, cuts little ice with modern congregations. The first verse of this hymn, for example, might well be omitted, thus giving the hymn a more distinguished title-line: 'Tis the spring of souls today'. In verse 3, line 5 (in SP)—'Comes to gladden Christian men'—I also prefer Dearmer's emendation of the last word to 'folk', to be inclusive. These slight adjustments, and the restoration of Neale's final stanza, would do no damage to this great hymn and could only add to the power of its message to today's world.

Awake, arise! Life up thy voice, from Christopher Smart's poem 'Easter Day', published in 1765, first appeared as a hymn in *Songs of Praise*. Surprisingly, subsequent compilers have ignored it. This highly original poet proclaims the Easter message with a refreshing turn of phrase. I like these verses:

And even as John, who ran so well,
   Confess upon our knees
The Prince who locks up death and hell
   And has himself the keys.

And thus through gladness and surprise
   The saints their Saviour treat;
Nor will they trust their ears and eyes
   But by his hands and feet.

The cento ends with powerful antitheses:

> O dead, arise, O friendless, stand
> By seraphim adored!
> O solitude, again command
> Thy host from heaven restored!

The tune St Fulbert suits these words well. Gauntlett wrote it in 1852 for another hymn and named it St Leofred. In A&M (1861) it was set to 'Ye choirs of new Jerusalem' and renamed *St Fulbert* after the author of the Latin words. Reading Robert Campbell's translation (A&M 73), one wonders what such phrases as 'new Jerusalem', 'Paschal victory', 'Judah's lion', 'serpent's head' and 'ransomed hosts' mean to modern congregations. Faced with the choice, I should have no hesitation in preferring Smart's thoroughly New Testament hymn as more helpful to worshippers of the present day.

The Easter hymns discussed here are samples of the standard repertoire. Among comparative newcomers, Percy Dearmer in 'A brighter dawn is breaking' (NEH 102) sees Easter as the dawn of a new age. In 'Thine be the glory' (A&M 428, NEH 120), a Swiss pastor takes us personally to the empty tomb and introduces us to the risen Master. Ada Habershon, in 'Jesus himself drew near' (AH 186), tells the Emmaus story with the refrain, 'Draw near, O Lord'. 'Walking in a garden' (A&M 518, NEH 123), by Father Hilary Greenwood, is worth its place for its last line, 'Only death is dead'.

HE ASCENDED INTO HEAVEN. It is generally understood that, just as Heaven is a state rather than a place, so the ascension of Jesus Christ should be thought of not in a geographical sense but as a change of status. In hymns, as in scripture, such figurative language as 'above the skies', 'on the clouds', 'above the starry height', is inevitable as a poetic picture of the return of Christ to glory after the humiliation of Bethlehem and Calvary. It would be a tragedy if the present vogue for eliminating everything that cannot be taken literally were to deprive us of our Ascensiontide hymns, and perhaps of belief in the ascension altogether. The time is ripe for a new appreciation of the poetry of the Bible and of the fact that much of it is reflected in the hymn book.

Hail the day that sees him rise. Like its sister hymn for Easter Day, Wesley's Ascension Day hymn has been shortened. Six of the original ten stanzas of 'Hail the day' are given in A&M, but a number of lines have been altered, chiefly by Thomas Cotterill in 1820. As these emendations are in the spirit of Wesley and for the most part improvements, we may as well take the hymn as it stands in A&M. The original in full is given in *The Penguin Book of Hymns.*

There is less scripture here than in the Easter hymn, but verse 2 is a good example of the same method of using it. Each of the two successive rhyming couplets consists of a statement of faith, followed by a scriptural exclamation, the latter introduced so spontaneously as to appear the natural consequence of the former. In this verse the passage thus used is Psalm 24:7:

> There for him high triumph waits;
> Lift your heads, eternal gates!
> He hath conquered death and sin;
> Take the King of glory in!

Wesley's original third line, 'Wide unfold the radiant scene' is better. The fifth verse is an amalgam of Hebrews 7:25, John 14:2 and 1 Corinthians 15:20. In the last (his eighth) Wesley shows himself a true Anglican by echoing the Prayer Book collect for Ascension Day.

See the conqueror mounts in triumph. Christopher Wordsworth (1807–85), nephew of Wordsworth the poet, was one of those gifted and co-ordinated people who excel at all they attempt. At school he distinguished himself on the playing-field as well as in class. After a brilliant academic career he was ordained. A canonry of Westminster followed in 1844. At the age of 43 he accepted a small Berkshire living where he remained a devoted parish priest and wrote a good deal until his elevation to the bishopric of Lincoln in 1869. In *The Holy Year* (1862) he set himself the task of providing a proper hymn for every Sunday and holy day as well as other occasions, after the example of Heber. Although Christopher Wordsworth had not the poetic gifts of Heber, his classical scholarship ensured a command of prosody. His hymns contain much teaching. Of the five verses of this one in A&M 88, verse 3, beginning 'He has raised our human nature', and verse 4, 'See him who is gone before us', sum up the scriptural doctrine of the ascension. After this no doxology is needed.

The head that once was crowned with thorns. Thomas Kelly was a prolific and highly successful hymn-writer. This, from his *Hymns on Various Passages of Scripture* (fifth edition, 1820) is based on Hebrew 2:10. The first line, as Percy Dearmer pointed out, is borrowed from John Bunyan.

FROM THENCE HE SHALL COME TO JUDGE ... The Second Coming has not been a popular theme with either preachers or hymn-writers for the past hundred years or so. The neglect of this article of faith may account not only for the Church's losing its sense of direction but also for the upsurge of bizarre sects which distort the doctrine into a heresy. Eighteenth-century divines had no such doubts or inhibitions.

Lo! He comes in clouds descending. In 1750 John Cennick, of Bohemian stock, wrote a hymn in six verses, beginning:

> Lo! He cometh, countless trumpets
> Blow before his bloody sign!

It depicts, with the downright directness characteristic of that age, the terrifying spectacle of the pierced and bruised Messiah sorting out his friends from his enemies. The sixth verse begins:

> View him smiling, now determined
> Every evil to destroy!

Language of this kind was not uncommon in the eighteenth century; but it was too much for Charles Wesley, who after Cennick's death rewrote the hymn in four stanzas. Wesley's version is virtually a new hymn; nothing of Cennick's remains but the metre. This is the version generally sung today, with the exception of the last two lines:

> Jah, Jehovah,
> Everlasting God, come down.

Methodists today retain these lines, substituting 'Come, Lord Jesus' for 'Jah, Jehovah'. NEH, and the latest URC and Baptist hymn-books, give Cennick's:

> O come quickly,
> Alleluia! Come, Lord, come.

AH mixes the two:

> O come quickly,
> Everlasting God, come down.

It also includes Cennick's best verse, beginning:

> Now redemption, long expected.
> See in solemn pomp appear,

with its reference to 1 Thesalomians 4:17.

The most powerful and positive ending to the hymn is that in A&M (1875 and subsequent editions), based on Revelation 19:6 and 11:15:

> Alleluia!
> Thou shalt reign, and thou alone.

At the name of Jesus. The whole credal teaching about Jesus Christ from creation to his return as judge is comprehended in this hymn. God's unique intervention in human history is described by St Paul (Philippians 2:5–11) and the fourth Evangelist (John 1:1–14). Caroline Noel has used these two passages as the basis of her finest hymn. The last line of the first stanza, 'Who from the beginning was the mighty Word', reminds her of the prologue to the fourth Gospel. After a second stanza which is never sung, it sparks off the train of thought that the babe of Bethlehem is lord and creator of all the powers of the universe: the stars in their courses, angels, spirits and all living creatures. Then, returning to the Philippians passage, the author interprets the poetry of St Paul in a flight of inspiration which soars beyond the great apostle himself:

> Humbled for a season, to receive a name
> From the lips of sinners unto whom he came,
> Faithfully he bore it spotless to the last,
> Brought it back victorious, when from death he passed:

Bore it up triumphant with its human light,
Through all ranks of creatures, to the central height,
To the throne of Godhead, to the Father's breast;
Filled it with the glory of that perfect rest.

In these two stanzas English hymnody reaches a high-water mark. But the whole hymn is lofty in theme and language. It makes no concessions to those who would play down the scriptural claim that Jesus is God.

I BELIEVE IN THE HOLY GHOST ... For many years Keble's 'When God of old came down from heaven' and Harriet Auber's 'Our blest Redeemer, ere he breathed' were the only hymns of teaching on the Holy Spirit in common use. They are now sung less, partly perhaps because exciting new ones have taken their places.

Our Lord, his Passion ended (A&M 91), written by Professor Burkitt in 1920, describes the Holy Spirit as firing with bravery and enthusiasm all who have witnessed for Christ from his first apostles to those of today. The change of metre from iambic to trochaic in the second half of each verse may well symbolise the change of direction inspired by the Spirit. This hymn, to Harold Darke's fine tune, deserves to be widely sung.

On the day of Pentecost (A&M 504). Here T. C. Hunter Clare deals with the same subject. It is significant that he too has adopted a metre which changes the accent; this is the last line of each quatrain. Patricia Hunt, in 'Upon the day of Pentecost', tells the story more concisely: see the Methodist hymn-book, *Hymns and Psalms* 328.

There's a spirit in the air (A&M 515). Brian Wren characteristically associates the Holy Spirit with feeding the hungry, housing the homeless and generally righting wrongs. As each verse is rounded off with a refrain there is no need to repeat verse 1 at the end.

Sing to him in whom creation (NEH 142), written by Michael Hewlett for EP 1975, is wide in its scope and clear in its teaching, linking Bible references from Genesis to Acts. It is also a useful processional.

Christians, lift up your hearts (A&M 444). Here John E. Bowers, whose distinguished contribution to English hymnody we have already noted, has provided another new Whitsuntide processional, full of praise, prayer and sound teaching, in the elegiac metre of *Salve feta dies* to carry Vaughan William's stirring tune.

THE HOLY CATHOLIC CHURCH ... Samuel John Stone published **The Church's one foundation** in 1866 at the age of 27, when he was curate of Windsor. Two years later he made minor improvements to the text and reduced it from seven stanzas to five for publication in the Appendix to A&M. In this form it has won deserved fame. No editor has altered a word.

Full of sound scriptural doctrine, this hymn affirms the teaching of the Apostles' Creed on the Church. It is holy, because its foundation is Christ (1 Corinthians 3:11), and it is 'his new creation by water and the word', that is, by his baptism and preaching. This has the authority of St Paul: 'Christ loved the Church and gave himself up for her, having cleansed her by the washing of water with the word' (Ephesians 5:26, RSV). The Church's relationship to Christ is in fact that of a bride to her husband—a figure from Revelation 21, the passage that had inspired the author of *Urbs beata* over a thousand years before. Also the Church is catholic:

> Elect from every nation,
> Yet one o'er all the earth.

The rest of that verse is derived from Ephesians 4:4–6, except for the line, 'Partakes one holy food', which has sufficient authority elsewhere.

Then come two stanzas which are as poignant as they are unexpected. The Church is in schism. This tragedy was nothing new in the 1860s. Heresy on the one hand, obscurantism on the other, have hindered the advance of God's kingdom down the ages and are with us today. The abrupt transition from apotheosis to lament in this hymn reminds us of the sudden humbling of the Church's foremost founder member after his triumphant confession at Caesarea Philippi. It has ever been thus with the Church, for though she is divine, as created by Christ and inhabited by the Holy Spirit, she is also human and therefore fallible. In that she is human, her progress is hindered by human conflict; but in that she is holy and in communion with the Church in heaven, her ultimate victory is assured. On this triumphant note the hymn ends.

The Church of God a kingdom is. The literary excellence and doctrinal soundness of this hymn by Lionel Muirhead are vouched for by its inclusion by Robert Bridges in the *Yattendon Hymnal.* Here again the theme is the holy catholic Church and the communion of saints, but its value is increased by the emphasis it lays upon the sacramental aspect of the Church's life and witness.

THE COMMUNION OF SAINTS ... I have chosen the hymn **Palms of glory, raiment bright** partly because it is a favourite of mine and partly for its symmetry and compactness (both of which are enhanced by the unanimous editorial omission of James Montgomery's penultimate stanza). Theologically the hymn is in line with the Reformed attitude to the saints as pointers to Christ rather than objects of veneration. Verse 1 begins with a procession of emblems:

> Palms of glory, raiment bright,
> Crowns that never fade away,
> Gird and deck the saints in light:
> Priests and kings and conquerors they.

The last line gives the groups of saints which the emblems represent: crowns for kings, 'raiment bright' for priests, palms for conquerors. In the three succeeding verses each group in turn casts its emblems before the Lamb, as in Revelation 7:9–15, attributing all their virtue to him. Finally we are reminded that the saints, like us, were sinners; but decked in Christ's righteousness, and 'translated thus', we too may triumph as conquerors, reign as kings and shine as priests.

The word 'saint' is commonly used to denote particular individuals: St Peter, St Andrew, St Mary. But in the words of St Paul all Christians are 'called to be saints'. A modern children's hymn that makes this point in a refreshing way is Lesbia Scott's 'I sing a song of the saints of God'—*The Hymnal* (USA, 1940) and *The BBC Hymn Book*. The last four lines will suffice to indicate its general tone:

You can meet them in school, or in lanes, or at sea,
In church, or in trains, or in shops, or at tea,
For the saints of God are just like me,
And I mean to be one too.

Let saints on earth in concert sing. Methodists know this hymn on the oneness of the Church on earth and within the veil as 'Come, let us join our friends above', the first of Wesley's original 40 lines; they sing 32 of them. Anglicans generally prefer the A&M version: five four-line stanzas beginning 'Let saints on earth'. Wesley's first four lines are omitted and ten of the rest altered. The essence of the hymn, however, is in the ten lines that have remained as Wesley wrote them:

For all the servants of our King
In heaven and earth are one.

One family we dwell in him,
One Church above, beneath;
Though now divided by the stream,
The narrow stream of death.

One army of the living God,
To his command we bow;
Part of his host have crossed the flood,
And part are crossing now.

The rare result of these many alterations is a fine, compact hymn, now widely sung in Britain and America.

He wants not friends that hath thy love. These six stanzas are from a longer poem by Richard Baxter, dated 1663, the year after his enforced separation from the Church of England. These lines reflect the thoughts that comforted him at that difficult time:

In the communion of saints
Is wisdom, safety and delight;
And when my heart declines and faints,
It's raised by their heart and light.

As for my friends, they are not lost;
The several vessels of thy fleet,

Though parted now, by temptest tost,
  Shall safely in the haven meet.

Still we are centred all in thee,
  Members, though distant, of one head;
In the same family we be,
  By the same faith and spirit led.

Before thy throne we daily meet
  As joint petitioners to thee;
In spirit we each other greet,
  And shall again each other see.

Though addressed to God, the lines are clearly intended to enlighten the reader. In no other hymn is the doctrine of the communion of saints more movingly expressed. Gibbon's tune, Angel's Song (NEH 235), suits these words well.

THE FORGIVENESS OF SINS, THE RESURRECTION OF THE BODY, AND THE LIFE EVERLASTING. The last three credal statements may be said to be the manward counterparts of the three great acts of Jesus Christ which the Creed states earlier: 'Was crucified, dead and buried ... The third day he rose again from the dead; He ascended into heaven ...' The Christian doctrine of the forgiveness of sins being centred on the cross, hymns on the Passion of our Lord are relevant. Many of these are discussed in other parts of this book.

It is a pity that the distaste for 'blood theology', which became fashionable in the first half of this century, deprived many worshippers of Cowper's 'There is a fountain filled with blood' and Wesley's

And can it be that I should gain
  An interest in the Saviour's blood?
Died he for me, who caused his pain?
  For me, who him to death pursued?
Amazing love! how can it be
  That thou, my God, should die for me?

There are now welcome signs of a revival of these hymns. When the Church can sing such hymns as these—and James Montgomery's 'Come let us sing the song of songs'—with some of the glowing conviction of their authors, it will have converting power in the present age. Young people have little patience with respectability. They want the truth, even though it shocks.

Forgive our sins as we forgive. This is another side to forgiveness. We often hear people say 'I can never forgive so-and-so.' And we can sympathise. Some things are hard to forgive. Most of the wars in the world today are due to this attitude. Yet our Lord taught us to pray 'Forgive us ... as we forgive'. Rosamond Herklots has given us a timely reminder in this hymn. Every Church should sing it.

As teaching on the forgiveness of sins is to be found in Passiontide hymns, so for teaching on the resurrection of the body we can turn to Easter hymns. Christ rose again because he was free from sin. Man's resurrection, therefore, is consequent upon forgiveness of sins through Jesus Christ. This is the teaching of St Paul in Romans 6 and 8, and it is echoed by the writers of Easter hymns in all ages. By St John of Damascus in the eighth century:

> All the winter of our sins,
> Long and dark, is flying,
> From his light, to whom we give
> Laud and praise undying.

By the German, Michael Weisse, in the sixteenth:

> Now he bids us tell abroad
> How the lost may be restored,
> How the penitent forgiven,
> How we too may enter heaven. Alleluia!

By our own Charles Wesley in the eighteenth:

> Soar we now where Christ has led,
> Following our exalted head;
> Made him like, like him we rise;
> Ours the cross, the grave, the skies.

But if I had to choose one hymn to express the doctrine of the resurrection of the body it would be that of Christian Gellert: **Jesus lives!** Gellert was a professor of philosophy and poetry at Leipzig, where he taught Goethe. The popular English version is by Frances Elizabeth Cox. Though in its present form abridged, the translation is faithful and conveys the spirit of the German, which rings with conviction. 'Alleluia' is not in the original, Gellert's triumphant refrain being '*Dies ist meine Zuversicht*' 'This is my trust'. It is on record that when told he had only one more hour to live, Gellert exclaimed, 'Now God be praised—only an hour!'

Now is eternal life (A&M 402), a valuable hymn by G.W. Briggs, declares that eternal life can begin here. It is all teaching, though the author turns aside to address God in verse 2 and Christ in verse 4, where he cites Romans 8:39 and Colossians 3:3.

The life of the world to come, as depicted in some of our hymns, is hardly a prospect that twentieth-century man can view with enthusiasm. This is understandable, since many hymn-writers have based their description of heaven on the extravagant imagery of apocalyptic vision. St Bernard of Cluny, for instance, founded his great poem, *Hora novissima*, from which 'Jerusalem the golden' is taken, on the last two chapters of Revelation:

> With jasper glow thy bulwarks,
> Thy streets with emeralds blaze,
> The sardine and the topaz
> Unite in thee their rays;
> Thine ageless walls are bonded
> With amethyst unpriced;
> Thy saints build up its fabric,
> The corner-stone is Christ.

Mrs Alexander's hymn 'The roseate hues of early dawn' is no longer sung, but one couplet still provides a household word:

> O for the pearly gates of heaven,
> O for the golden floor.

Even James Montgomery in his beautiful hymn 'For ever with the Lord' cannot lose sight of 'the golden gates'; and Samuel Crossman in 'Jerusalem on high' holds out the spectacle of 'the bleeding martyrs' as a thing 'I might with joy behold'. Peter Abelard, however, is more inviting in *O quanta qualia*—'O what their joy and their glory must be':

Wish and fulfilment can severed be ne'er,
Nor the thing prayed for come short of the prayer.

And Thomas a Kempis in *Jerusalem luminosa*—'Light's abode, celestial Salem'—has the radiant stanza:

O how glorious and resplendent
Fragile body, shalt thou be,
When endued with so much beauty,
Full of health and strong and free,
Full of vigour, full of pleasure
That shall last eternally!

This glowing description of the resurrection body, translated by J.M. Neale, has the authority of St Paul in Philippians 3:21.

There is a land of pure delight. A picture of heaven we can all appreciate is that which is said to have inspired Isaac Watts as he stood one summer evening gazing across Southampton Water (says a biographer, T. Wright) at the 'swelling uplands and ample meadows which stretch beyond as far even as the waving masses of the New Forest'.

There everlasting spring abides,
And never-withering flowers;
Death, like a narrow stream, divides
That heavenly land from ours.

Sweet fields beyond the swelling flood
Stand dressed in living green;
So to the Jews old Canaan stood,
While Jordan rolled between.

How refreshing to come across this robust open-air hymn, which likens the abode of God to the nearest thing we have to heaven on earth—the countryside!

THE CHURCH CATECHISM, which enshrines the fundamental teaching of our religion, deals not only with the Creed but also with Christian conduct, prayer and sacraments. We need a hymn on the ten commandments, expressing them positively and relating them to the Christian law of love (Romans 3:10). Such a hymn David Mowbray has provided in **Father**

of all, whose laws have stood (HTC 539). It aptly describes the commandments as 'signposts for man's earthly good'; each verse ends with a prayer based on Ephesians 3:18. The first four commandments are implied in verse 2, the fifth and seventh in verse 3, the sixth, ninth and tenth in verse 4. As each verse is rounded off with a refrain, the hymn is sufficiently balanced without the repetition of verse 1 at the end. Norman Cocker's tune fits these words well and should impress them on the memory.

THE DIFFICULTY OF PRAYER is recognised in **What various hindrances we meet** and **Prayer is the soul's sincere desire.** The former was written by William Cowper at Olney for use at the rector's weekly prayer meeting (see chapter 4); the latter, by James Montgomery, we have discussed in chapter 2. But as Cowper points out, the problem does not arise when we grumble:

> Have we no words? Ah, think again,
> Words flow apace when we complain
> And fill our fellow creatures' ear
> With the sad tale of all our care.

And prayer is the best antidote:

> Were half the breath thus vainly spent
> To heaven in supplication sent,
> Our cheerful song would oftener be
> 'Hear what the Lord has done for me'.

For Montgomery, however, there are times when words are not needed:

> Prayer is the burden of a sigh,
> The falling of tear,
> The upward glancing of an eye
> When none but God is near.

And even the 'simplest form of speech' becomes sublime when uttered in prayer.

The omission of both of these hymns from one important modern hymnal leaves a regrettable gap, and necessitates the overworking of another of Montgomery's hymns, 'Lord, teach us how to pray aright', which does not cover the same ground, being itself a prayer for grace to pray.

AS MOST HYMNS ON BAPTISM AND HOLY COMMUNION are addressed to God and are discussed in other parts of this book, I need here mention only two: Dean Alford's classic, 'In token that thou shalt not fear', based on the words of the baptism service at the signing of the cross (A&M 424); and William Bright's scholarly communion hymn, 'Once, only once, and once for all', in which he summarizes NT eucharistic teaching. Christ sacrificed himself once for all upon the cross for the salvation of the world (Hebrews 10:1). Although this offering is complete and cannot be repeated, it is shown forth perpetually in this service (1 Corinthians 11:26). At every Eucharist the Church, assembled at his command, is identified with Christ and offered by him on heaven's eternal throne. In the same mystic rite Christ gives himself to the faithful.

There are of course many more hymns addressed to the worshipper on every aspect of Christian belief. The foregoing have been selected to support my contention that not all hymns are addressed to God in praise or prayer. Many are addressed to us. Like the scriptures, they were 'written for our learning'. Indeed, on a desert island—without even the proverbial Bible one might learn the Christian faith from a good hymn book.

6 HYMNS ADDRESSED TO US ABOUT OURSELVES: EXHORTATION

THE HYMNS WE ARE ABOUT TO DISCUSS are neither directly addressed to God nor primarily about God. Their subject is human life and behaviour, their purpose exhortation. Nevertheless most of them are based on scripture and may therefore be understood as God speaking to us.

'FOLLOW ME.' It was the first command of Christ. To those who obeyed, it meant giving up the security of the world and trusting Christ completely; it might also mean self-denial and suffering. Several hymn-writers have taken up this theme.

Jesus calls us! o'er the tumult. Mrs Alexander founded this hymn on Matthew 4:18–22, the Gospel for St Andrew's Day. It was clearly intended for use on that day, since Andrew is singled out, although Peter, James and John were called at the same time; but it was also suitable for general use.

Three Gospel calls are brought to mind: the calling of the rich young man (Mark 10:21,22) in verse 3, and the risen Lord's searching question and commission to Peter (John 21:15) in verse 4. In the last passage the Greek for 'more than these' is as ambiguous as the English: it could mean 'more than these people' or 'more than these things'. Did Jesus mean, 'Do you love me more than these other disciples do?' or 'Do you love me more than fishing?' Most New Testament commentators have preferred the former, but Mrs Alexander has assumed the latter reading, which certainly seems the more reasonable. Only the night before, Peter had implied his intention of returning to the fishing industry. Even as Jesus spoke, the boat and its tackle were lying on the shore in full view. 'If you love me more than these things,' says Jesus, 'leave them and work for me.' This tallies with Mark 10:28–30. The theme of the hymn is that, in a clash of loyalties between Jesus and the world, the Christian should choose Jesus.

Take up thy cross, the Saviour said. One would scarcely take this solemn hymn for the work of a teenager. The young

American, Charles William Everest, was 19 years old when he published *Visions of Death and Other Poems*, including this, in 1833. Later he was ordained priest and spent his entire ministry in the same district of Connecticut. Based on Christ's challenge in Mark 8:34, 'Whosoever will come after me, let him deny himself, take up his cross and follow me', these verses deal with some of the ogres of the Christian life: pride, temptation, fear of commitment.

During Everest's lifetime the hymn was much altered: who made the changes is not known, and not all of them are for the better. On the positive side, in the third line of verse 1, where Everest merely repeats 'Take up thy cross', the change to 'Deny thyself' is a great gain, being in line with our Lord's words. And in verse 5, 'follow Christ' is more explicit than the author's 'follow on'. On the other side, the original ends powerfully with that fifth verse: the added doxology is superfluous. Moreover, in verse 2 I prefer the original second line, 'Fill thy weak soul with vain alarm'. If we follow Christ, alarm is indeed vain. Above all, in the third line of verse 1 again, neither Everest nor Jesus Christ said 'the world forsake'. (Everest's original line was 'Take up thy cross with willing heart'.) It is in 1 John 2:15 that we are bidden 'Love not the world'; and this cannot mean the world of humanity, which 'God so loved', but the desires of the world. Sebastian Temple's modern hymn, 'Follow Christ and love the world as he did' (CCH 76), is sound scriptural advice.

Happy are they, they that love God. The refreshing thing about this hymn is that it dwells upon the sheer joy of following Christ. Public worship, private prayer, home life, even suffering and death, are steeped in happiness. It might be described as a rhapsody on two texts: 'My yoke is easy' and 'All things work together for good to them that love God'. It springs from one of the Latin hymns which Charles Coffin wrote for the Paris Breviary in 1736, '*O quam juvat fratres, Deus*'. John Chandler loosely translated in 1837 as 'O Lord, how joyful 'tis to see'. Robert Bridges, as we have already observed, often wrote hymns to revive the use of old tunes; 'Happy are they' is a case in point. He began it with the object of providing a translation of *O quam juvat* that would carry the tune Binchester by William Croft. The happy melody so spurred him that he soon forgot the Latin and produced a new hymn.

Jesus bids us shine. Portia, in *The Merchant of Venice*, says:

> How far that little candle throws his beams!
> So shines a good deed in a naughty world.

Less poetic but equally apt is this simple hymn by Susan Warren, based on Matthew 5:16, published in America in 1868 and popularised in this country by Moody and Sankey. Though its first verse is still a household word and the whole lyric is in the *Penguin Book of Hymns*, it has been dropped by the latest editions of all our standard hymnals. Perhaps it is outshone by Kendrick's *Shine, Jesus, shine*, which though addressed to Christ, has the same message. By all means let Kendrick be sung today: but will his words be remembered for a hundred years? Susan Warner's have been.

Ye servants of the Lord. Dr Philip Doddridge (1702–1751), a distinguished Congregationalist minister, would often write a hymn on the subject of his sermon and have it sung at the close of the service. The problem of having it printed in time did not arise, because in those days each line of a hymn was read out before it was sung. 'Ye servants of the Lord' was written to follow a sermon on the second coming of Christ, the text being Luke 12:35–38. It is a good hymn, as one expects of Doddridge, but it amounts to little more than a free paraphrase of the passage. It does not tell the modern Christian how to obey the command 'Watch'. Presumably 'Observant of his heavenly word' means studying the Bible. But how do we trim our lamps, gird our loins, or 'mark the first signal of his hand'? For the answer we must turn to our next hymn.

Awake, my soul, and with the sun, part 1, is entirely hortatory. This was Bishop Ken's advice to the Winchester boys of the seventeenth century:

> Redeem thy mis-spent time that's past,
> Live this day as if 'twere thy last:
> Improve thy talent with due care;
> For the great day thyself prepare.

Let all thy converse be sincere,
Thy conscience as the noon-day clear;
Think how all-seeing God thy ways
And all thy secret thoughts surveys.

By influence of the light divine
Let thy own light in good works shine;
Reflect all heaven's propitious ways
In ardent love and cheerful praise.

'BE A PILGRIM.' Christians from earliest times have spoken of life's journey as a pilgrimage and of themselves as pilgrims. 'Here we have no continuing city, but we seek one to come', says the writer to the Hebrews; 'Our citizenship is in heaven' writes St Paul; and St Peter addresses his converts as 'strangers and pilgrims'. According to the New Testament the Christian is not at home on earth; his aim is to reach heaven. This is the theme of James Montgomery's hymn, **For ever with the Lord**. The title line is from 1 Thessalonians 4:17, and the second half of the first verse is based on 2 Corinthians 5:6, 8. This beautiful hymn, like Cennick's 'Children of the heavenly King', is less sung than it used to be. People today are more interested in improving conditions in this world than in pressing on to the next. There is certainly an element of unreality about folk in the prime of life standing up and virtually praying for an early death. Other hymns in which the hope of heaven is held out as a spur to greater efforts in this life have held their place better.

Through the night of doubt and sorrow. Bernhardt Ingemann (1789–1862) wrote this hymn, which was included in the *Danish Hymnal* and later translated into English by Sabine Baring-Gould. Its theme is the brotherhood and unity of the Christian Church. Martin Shaw's vigorous tune Marching has contributed to its popularity, as has also the omission of the last two quatrains, which take the 'pilgrim band' no farther than the 'far eternal shore' already reached in verse 6.

Who would true valour see. This apotheosis of the pilgrim life was inserted by John Bunyan into the second edition of *Pilgrim's Progress*. Its open-air directness appeals to young and old alike. But it would probably never have been sung as a hymn had it not been rewritten by Percy Dearmer for EH as 'He who would valiant be'. The superb tune Monk's Gate, made by Vaughan Williams from a Sussex folk song, has ensured its popularity. Once the hymn thus became established, purists began to criticise Dearmer for altering the words, and it was included in other hymn books more or less as Bunyan wrote it. Dearmer tells the whole story in *Songs of Praise Discussed*. There are advantages in either version, but credit must go to EH for introducing this stirring hymn and tune to the Christian world.

He that is down need fear no foe. From the same source, this is the song of a poor shepherd boy overheard by Mr Greatheart and his companions in the Valley of Humiliation. After they had listened to the song their guide said: 'I will dare to say that this boy lives a merrier life and wears more of that herb called Heart's ease in his bosom that he that is clad in scarlet and velvet.'

Rise in the strength of God. Ada Randall Greenaway contributed several hymns to A&M, including this one on the text. 'They that wait upon the Lord shall renew their strength' from Isaiah 40:31. Sir Sydney Nicholson's tune Totteridge, with its change of time in the third line, not only fits the words exactly but adds to their grit and air of confidence. It is appropriate as a post-communion hymn.

'FIGHT.' We come now to a group of hymns urging the Christian to fight evil. Their writers seized on the Pauline metaphor of the Christian as a soldier and hence the Church as an army. On the one hand these hymns have been criticised for being militarist. F.R. Barry declared in 1931 that there was nothing in the whole world that the Church should less resemble than an army. On the other hand there are those in more recent times who regard it as the Church's duty to encourage and take part in the physical overthrow of established regimes which they consider corrupt. This is perhaps the opinion given voice by Fred Kaan in his version of the *Magnificat*, 'Sing we a song a high revolt' (A&M 419).

The Christian soldiers of the New Testament, however, are

not concerned with the overthrow of temporal power. 'My kingdom is not of this world,' said Jesus. 'Render to Ceaser the things that are Caesar's.' His followers are called to 'endure hardness' and be disciplined (2 Timothy 2:3, 4). 'For our fight is not against human foes, but against the superhuman forces of evil in the heavens' (Ephesians 6:12, NEB.). The Christian's weapons are not guns and bombs but 'the whole armour of God'. And it is this spiritual warfare which is referred to in the old fighting hymns we are about to consider.

Soldiers of Christ, arise. The five or six four-line verses now usually sung are no more than fragments of Charles Wesley's original hymn, which had twelve eight-line stanzas and was divided into three equal parts. It is not a paraphrase of Ephesians 6:10–18, but an impassioned exhortation drawing freely on material from that passage. Wesley's first two stanzas became verses 1, 2, 3 and 5 in the EH version, verse 4 of which is the first quatrain of the original twelfth. The verse beginning 'To keep your armour bright' in AH is the first half of Wesley's seventh stanza. *The Methodist Hymn Book* includes another stanza:

> Leave no unguarded place,
> No weakness of the soul;
> Take every virtue, every grace,
> And fortify the whole:
> Indissolubly joined,
> To battle all proceed;
> But arm yourselves with all the mind
> That was in Christ, your head.

In *Christian Worship*, a Free Church hymnal published in 1975, Howard Mudditt, the editor, gives five eight-line verses, including one too long neglected that begins 'Pray without ceasing, pray'. They are all set out as Wesley wrote them, except one in which quatrains from two different stanzas have been combined. Some such piecing together is essential in reducing a hymn of this length to singable proportions. Here is another quatrain that might well be revived:

But above all, lay hold
On faith's victorious shield:
Armed with that adamant of gold,
Be sure to win the field.

There is ample material for a cento of six eight-line verses. For practical purposes they might be arranged in three parts. One or two parts could then be used as occasion demanded; or the whole, sung to a tune in double short metre, would make a fine processional. Edward Naylor's tune From Strength to Strength shows the right way; some day, perhaps, it will be bettered.

Onward, Christian soldiers. This marching song of the Church was written by Sabine Baring-Gould in 1865 while he was in charge of a mission church at Horbury Bridge in Yorkshire. It was intended for an open-air Sunday-school procession. In those days the use of a processional cross was considered very high-church. Some editors therefore altered the last line of the refrain to 'Looking unto Jesus, who is gone before' and the first line of the second verse to 'At the name of Jesus Satan's host doth flee'. The latter survives in AH. The compilers of the ill-fated 1904 edition of A&M altered 'We are not divided, all one body we' to 'Though divisions harass, all one body we', and persuaded the septuagenarian author to agree that their emendation was more realistic. But the public rejected both the emendation and the book in which it appeared. Indeed, the hymn is so well known that any alteration would be noticed immediately.

One cannot consider this famous hymn apart from the tune, St Gertrude. It was for the musical edition of the *Hymnary* 1872 that Joseph Barnby asked his friend, Arthur Sullivan, to set these words. Shortly afterwards Sullivan handed him the manuscript of St Gertrude and said, 'Will this do?' What it has done is to immortalise the hymn. Various attempts have been made to supplant it, but to no avail. Recently I asked the headmaster of a large primary school if the school ever sang 'Onward, Christian soldiers' to St Gertrude. He replied, 'It's top of the pops.'

Fight the good fight. Writing to Timothy in the heydey of the Roman empire, when soldiers tramped the streets of every city, St Paul said, 'Fight the good fight of faith' (1 Timothy 6:12). To the young church at Corinth, where contests between athletes drew great crowds, he wrote: 'Like them, run to win!' (1 Corinthians 9:25). His advice to the Philippians is 'Have no anxiety, but in everything make your requests known to God' (Philippians 4:6). And again to Timothy the old campaigner declares: 'I have fought a good fight, I have finished my course, I have kept the faith', and goes on to promise a crown of righteousness to those who are faithful to the end (2 Timothy 4:7, 8). The author of this hymn has combined these texts in four simple verses. John Samuel Bewley Monsell (1811–1875) was an Irish clergyman who served most of his ministry in England and was killed when masonry from the roof of his church, St Nicholas, Guildford fell on his head. His memorial is in his hymns.

Oft in danger, oft in woe. This is mainly the work of two young people. In 1805 Henry Kirk White, a brilliant undergraduate aged 20, was sitting in the examination room at Cambridge. Having finished his maths paper before time, he began to write this hymn on the back of it. He scribbled ten lines, left the paper behind, and died a few months later. This is what he had written:

> Much in sorrow, oft in woe,
> Onward, Christians, onward go,
> Fight the fight, and worn with strife,
> Steep with tears the bread of life.
>
> Onward, Christians, onward go,
> Join the war and face the foe,
> Faint not—much doth yet remain,
> Dreary is the long campaign.
>
> Shrink not, Christian, will ye yield?
> Will ye quit the painful field?

By one of those curious chances that may be described as providential this fragment was preserved and, years later, came into the hands of Bertha Fuller-Maitland, who was then compiling a hymn book. She showed it to her teenage daughter, Frances, remarking what a pity it was unfinished. Presently the girl brought her mother a further fourteen lines which she had written herself. The hymn, thus completed, was included in her mother's *Hymns for Private Devotion*, published in 1827. In 1833 Edward Bickersteth in his *Christian Psalmody* altered the first line to 'Oft in sorrow, oft in woe' and the rest of verse 1 to the form that is now familiar. In 1836 W.J. Hall in the *Mitre Hymn Book* added the finishing touch: by changing 'sorrow' to 'danger'. This is perhaps the most valuable emendation of all. First, it makes a more euphonious title line; second, whereas 'sorrow' and 'woe' are synonymous, 'danger' introduces a new element; and third it provides a sense of unity, since 'danger' is taken up again in verse 2 and 'woe' in verse 4.

The last four lines of the original fragment are never sung, and three of the first six have been altered, whereas Frances Fuller-Maitland's fourteen lines are sung in their entirety with only two inconsequential changes. Nevertheless our greatest gratitude must be to Henry Kirk White, but for whose scribbling we should never have had the hymn at all.

'YOU SHALL BE MY WITNESS': those words were the last marching orders to the apostles from Christ. This, then, is the Church's task. The command has been handed on by hymn-writers in various ways: 'Come, labour on,' says June Borthwick; 'Go, labour on' says Horatius Bonar. These two authors were born within five years of each other at the beginning of the nineteenth century, lived over eighty years in Edinburgh and were enthusiastic members of the Free Church of Scotland, of which Dr Bonar became Moderator. They must have met.

Stand up! stand up for Jesus. The story of how his hymn came to be written has been told many times. It is worth telling again, partly because it explains certain features of the hymn and partly because it vindicates the principle of the parson's freehold. Dudley Tyng was minister of a wealthy church in Philadelphia where he did not have a freehold; he was employed by the congregation. At that time, in the middle of the nineteenth century, slavery was still rife. Tyng denounced it in his sermons as evil. As most of his congregation were slave-owners this offended them, and Tyng was summoned before the elders and forbidden to preach on that subject again. He disregarded them, however, and was dismissed. But his friends, who believed in him, hired for his use the largest hall in Philadelphia and there he continued his ministry. Week by week the hall was packed; many were converted by his preaching. One day he was badly mangled by farm machinery and died a few hours later. When asked by a friend at his bedside if he had any message for his congregation, he said, 'Tell them to stand up for Jesus.' His friend, George Duffield, a Presbyterian minister, heard the message and wrote this hymn.

Verse 2 refers to the garden of Gethsemane where, it will be remembered, the disciples fell asleep at their prayers. In the anti-militarist years between the two world wars the Shakespearean phrase 'God of battles' was altered to 'God of freedom' (see SP 646). In verse 3 the line, 'Ye that are men now serve him' does not of course mean that women are precluded; it is a reference to the last sermon preached by Dudley Tyng, to a gathering of 5000 people the Sunday before he died, on the text 'Go now ye that are men, and serve the Lord' (Exodus 10:11). Verse 4 is founded on Ephesians 6:13–18, Dr Duffield's text for the funeral sermon, which he concluded by reciting this hymn. A verse referring to that particular occasion, and therefore now omitted, is worth quoting for its attitude to the loss of a valued leader:

> Stand up! stand up for Jesus!
> Each soldier to his post.
> Close up the broken column,
> And shout through all the host:
> Make good the loss so heavy
> In those that still remain;
> And prove to all around you
> That death itself is gain.

The tune Morning Light is by George James Webb (1803–1887), an Englishman who spent most of his life as an organist and teacher in America. The melody, originally composed for the secular song ' 'Tis dawn, the lark is singing' (hence its name), was soon adapted as a hymn-tune. It is a mission-hymn tune, simple, vigorous and ideally suited to these words, from which it is now inseparable.

Ye that know the Lord is gracious. Dr C.A. Alington, who became Dean of Durham in 1933 and died in 1955, wrote much—not only theology but poetry and novels as well. Among his hymns, two are now in frequent use and will probably continue to be sung in years to come: the Easter hymn, 'Good Christian men, rejoice and sing', and this one, addressed to the Church about its mission. I know of no other hymn that fills this niche. It is based on 1 Peter 2:1–10.

O Faith of England, taught of old (altered to 'Faith of our fathers'; NEH 479). This magnificent hymn by T.A. Lacey not only makes possible the use in this country of a noble sixteenth-century German tune in its original form, but also provides the Church with a stirring battle song. The first half of each stanza is a statement of Christian faith as taught and defended by the Church in all the ups and downs of her history. The second half, beginning with the refrain:

> Arise, arise good Christian men,
> Your glorious standard raise again,

is a rousing call to loyalty and witness in the present age. An occasional touch of healthy triumphalism such as this is a welcome offset to the death-wish expressed by certain Anglicans today.

'TEACH ALL NATIONS.' So radically has the situation in the overseas mission field changed in recent years that some of the finest missionary hymns have gone out of use. Two classics immediately spring to mind.

From Greenland's icy mountains was written by Reginald Heber in 1819 for a service in aid of the SPG in Wrexham Parish Church. The whole of the second stanza now has to be omitted because it is no longer true that 'The heathen in his blindness Bows down to wood and stone'. But the world still needs Christ, and the rest of the hymn is an eloquent and timely reminder of his command to 'preach the gospel to every creature'.

Hills of the North, rejoice. Charles Oakley wrote these verses shortly before his early death in 1865 at the age of 33. Like Heber, he saw the bounds of the Church's mission as extending to the four points of the compass. This is another hymn which, though too good to drop, contains details which can no longer truthfully be sung. The offending verse is the third, beginning 'Lands of the East, awake!' They are now wide awake, though not in the way we had hoped: China is a Communist state and Islam plans a mission for the conversion of England.

The editors of *English Praise* (1975) solved the problem by writing a new hymn which retains Oakley's first line and general pattern and, of course, Martin Shaw's tune Little Cornard. It reads well, but so radical a revision seems to me unnecessary. Only the third verse needed amendment.

Many of the best known missionary hymns are prayers and therefore do not lie within the scope of this chapter. But here are some hortative missionary hymns of a more general character that have stood the test of time; for example, Montgomery's 'Lift up your heads, ye gates of brass' and Bishop Doane's 'Fling out the banner'. Also there is 'God is working his purpose out', with its refrain from Habakkuk 2:14, by that scholar and much-loved master at Eton, Arthur Campbell Ainger (who also wrote the famous school song, *Carmen Etonense*, set to music by Sir Joseph Barnby). It will be noted that in each of these hymns the Church is pictured as an army with banners. There are also one or two in AH by more recent writers, notably 'Christ is the world's true light', by G.W. Briggs (NEH 494). It is significant that all these hymns are equally applicable to the scene. The distinction between home and foreign missions no longer exists.

THE CALL TO SOCIAL SERVICE is now often heard. The emphasis of the modern Church seems to be less on preaching the gospel than on putting it into practice. And this is reflected in hymns on human rights, race relations and world peace.

Anglican hymnals of the last century did not reflect the concern of forward-looking churchmen or social justice. The only hymn in A&M remotely connected with the subject was a period piece included in the Supplement of 1889 and (for reasons given in chapter 1) not removed until 1950. Even today some churches still use the old Standard Edition (1924), where this hymn appears under the heading (in Gothic type) 'For a Service for Working Men':

Sons of labour, dear to Jesus,
  To your homes and work again;
Go with brave hearts back to duty,
  Face the perils, bear the pain.
Be your dwellings ne'er so lowly
  Yet remember, by your bed,
That the Son of God most holy
  Had not where to lay his head.

There are six more stanzas in much the same strain. There is, however, one quatrain expressing the Christian attitude to work which it is only fair to quote:

Sons of labour, live for Jesus,
  Be your work your worship too;
In his name and to his glory
  Do whate'er you find to do.

S.R. Hole, the author, was Dean of Rochester and an authority on roses.

In our first chapter we noted four hymns of social concern introduced by EH 1906: 'Judge eternal', 'O God of earth and altar', 'When wilt thou save the people?' and 'Once to every man and nation'. The same editor, Percy Dearmer, included them in SP 1925 along with others, mostly under a social-services heading, notably 'Turn back, O man' by Clifford Bax and 'Father eternal, ruler of creation' by Laurence Housman. I heartily second Ian Bradley's plea (in *The Penguin Book of Hymns*) that these two should have wider currency. Indeed, I would add two centos: 'These things shall be', from J.A. Symonds', poem 'A Vista' and Whittier's lines 'O brother man, fold to thy heart thy brother'.

And did those feet in ancient time ...? Where do we place this timeless lyric? It is a national song rather than a hymn, but it is needed in hymn-books for use in church on certain occasions. Based as it is on the legend that Jesus Christ may have visited this country, its appeal is particularly to the English. Yet in the Albert Hall for the last night of the Proms there must be many Scots, Irish and Welsh singers caught up in the spirit of the song.

William Blake (1757–1827) was an original artist of spectacular imagination, a man born out of his time. He was virtually self-taught, the only school he attended being a drawing-school which he entered at the age of 10. At 14 he was apprenticed to an engraver and, at 21, started work as a freelance professional in that line. He also wrote poetry. As time went on he combined all three gifts in the production of his poems: he illustrated, engraved and printed them himself. These, his most famous lines, which we call 'Jerusalem', are not from Blake's great poem of that name, nor indeed are they an integral part of any of his major poetical works. They were an afterthought, tacked on to the preface to his poem 'Milton'.

Although this eighteenth-century mystic was an ardent apostle of freedom, what he wanted was freedom to develop the mind and imagination. The 'dark satanic mills' have nothing to do with the industrial revolution, but refer to the mills of formal education, based on the classics and logic, which in Blake's view obstructed imgination's flow. His 'bow of burning gold', 'arrows of desire', 'spear' and 'chariot of fire' probably symbolise the divine gift of his own genius. The Preface to 'Milton' ends: 'We do not want either Greek or Roman models if we are but just and true to our own imaginations, those worlds of eternity in which we shall live for ever in Jesus our Lord.' Then follow the sixteen famous lines. These details, however, are purely academic. Jerusalem is still the city of God, the body of Christ; in fact, the Church. It is to the building up of that body in England, until by the grace of God it fills the whole land with peace and goodwill, that Christians dedicate themselves in this song.

Another remarkable feature is the tune, without which 'Jerusalem' would never have been known. It was in the depressing early months of World War I that Robert Bridges, then Poet Laureate, saw the potential of these lines to inspire the right kind of patriotism and resolution. He asked Sir Hubert Parry to set them to simple music which a crowd could sing. Parry complied and gave his manuscript to Sir Walford Davies, who was much engaged with community singing at that time. It was published in 1916. Besides doing valuable war service, it figured in the suffragette movement and was later adopted by the Women's Institute. Today it is regarded as a second national anthem.

Among the changes of the Sixties was the way in which some of the new hymn-writers expressed their social concern. The heroic idealism of older writers gave place to the brash cynicism of, for example, Geoffrey Ainger's 'Now Dives was a charitable man', which my younger son remembers singing at school. More durable are the songs of Sydney Carter. Two of Carter's songs of social impact are certainly satirical; but his satire, as with Dickens or W.S. Gilbert, springs from situations and makes us laugh at ourselves.

No use knocking at the window (A&M 400) addresses two problems. One is social:

> We are Christian men and women,
> Always willing, never able.

The other is racial:

> In this house he will be welcome
> But we hope he won't be black, Sir.

The punch line thus:

> Till you woke us with your knocking
> We were sleeping like the dead, Sir.

In **When I needed a neighbour** (A&M 433) it is Christ who asks the questions (see Matthew 25:34–40) and who adds at the end: 'Wherever you may travel, I'll be there'.

We have already met Fred Kaan, Fred Pratt Green and Brian Wren and noted their concern with justice, race relations and world peace. Most of their hymns on these subjects are addressed to God or Jesus Christ. Some are suitable for services where members of differing churches meet to pray for unity. It was reported recently that at such a meeting delegates of all races, approaching the altar, spontaneously burst out singing the American spiritual 'Let us break bread together on our knees'.

Now let us from this table rise (A&M 403), another communion hymn by Fred Kaan, has the moving line, 'It is the sacrament of care'.

What Adam's disobedience cost (A&M 524). In considering social reform, we do well to remember that the Christian gospel proclaims more than reconciliation between man and man; it proclaims reconciliation between man and God. This is the key to all else. Pratt Green's carol is a timely reminder.

Life is great! So sing about it (A&M 482), writes Brian Wren. But he is careful to add in his final stanza:

> God is great! In Christ he loved us,
> As we should, but never can.

What does the Lord require for praise and offering? (A&M 432). Albert Bayly, whom we have also met before, answers the prophet's question in this hymn addressed to rulers, masters of wealth, merchants and workers. It is an eloquent sermon on his chosen text.

Before we take the body of our Lord (WS 8). John Bell and Graham Maule of the Iona Community, in what amounts to a self-examination before communion, remind us of social sins we should 'lay down' before Christ for forgiveness. The last verse is a prayer that he will replace them with his own presence and power.

'PRAISE THE LORD.' As we have already observed, certain important hymns are hard to place precisely in any of our four classes. Though in praise of God, they are addressed to the worshipper. Though about God, their teaching is incidental. Their theme is the duty and joy of thanksgiving. They stand in a class by themselves. The four verses of Psalm 100 alternate between exhortation to praise and teaching about God's love and providence as grounds for it. Watts ends his version with the two stanzas of direct praise which I quoted in Chapter 1. 'Praise the Lord, ye heavens adore him' (based on Psalm 148) and 'Let us with a gladsome mind' (Psalm 136) concentrate on the reasons for praise. In 'All creatures of our God and King'. W. H. Draper, following St Francis's Canticle of the Sun—and indeed the *Benedicite*—invites all creation, animate and inanimate, to praise the Lord. In 'Let all the world in every corner sing' Herbert calls upon heaven, earth, the Church and each individual to swell the chorus; in 'O praise ye the Lord', Sir Henry Baker asks for instrumental accompaniment. 'Ye holy angels bright', (written by Richard Baxter in 1672 and rewritten by J. Hampden Gurney in 1838), invokes angels, saints and the departed to assist our praises. Athelstan Riley's fine hymn, 'Ye watchers and ye holy ones', is in much the same strain; in verse 2, with a thinly veiled reference to the *Magnificat*, it enjoins the Mother of our Lord to lead the heavenly choir.

Nearer still to the borderline between exhortation and praise are three widely-sung hymns addressed to 'my soul'.

Praise to the Lord, the almighty, the King of creation. The seventeenth-century German hymn *Lobe den Herren* by Joachim Neander, with the tune adopted by him from an earlier hymn to suit his own words, is a favourite in Germany and Switzerland. It is based broadly on verses from Psalms 103 and 150. In Catherine Winkworth's translation (1863) it has become popular in this country and, sometimes altered, throughout the English-singing world.

Praise, my soul, the King of heaven. Henry Lyte's famous words are also from Psalm 103: verses 1 to 5 in his first stanza, verses 6–10 in his second, verses 13, 14, 11 and 12 in his third, and verses 20–22 in his fourth. It first appeared in Lyte's *Spirit of the Psalms* with a stanza on verse 16–19, bracketed by the author for omission, between our third and fourth. This stanza is never sung. Otherwise unaltered, 'Praise my soul' remains a choice distillation of the psalm. Goss's tune was, I believe, written at the request of Robert Brown-Borthwick, a noted musical priest who as Vicar of All Saints, Scarborough, established a musical tradition there which survived him for some thirty years.

Tell out, my soul, the greatness of the Lord. Timothy Dudley-Smith, later Bishop of Thetford, tells us (*Lift Every Heart*, 1984) that he had no thought of being a hymn-writer when he jotted down these verses on 19 May 1961 on first reading the NEB version of *Magnificat*. It was the editors of AH who asked if they might use them as a hymn. By 1983 it had appeared in over fifty collections. That number is still increasing. Of hymns written in the last three decades this must be the most widely sung. For a 'first fine careless rapture' it is a remarkably finished piece. By starting each stanza with the same four words the author gives it unity. By answering the first stanza in the last—recalling 'the promise of his word' and closing with an extension of his opening line—he gives it symmetry. Above all, by following NEB and omitting personal and national references, he enables twentieth-century worshippers to make the song of Mary their own.

A NOTE ON DOXOLOGIES, to conclude. The hymns discussed in this and the previous chapter are addressed to the worshipper. Their object is to teach or to exhort. Anglican readers, particularly users of A&M, may have wondered why many of them end with a doxology or prayer addressed to God.

The answer goes back to the fourth century, when the Christian doxology, *Gloria Patri*, was added to each of the psalms. The ancient Latin hymn-writers followed the same pattern, no doubt to guard against heresy. At the Reformation, Luther and his followers appended doxologies only to hymns based on the Old Testament or the Apocrypha. Thus Matin Rinkart's 'Now thank we all our God', being a paraphrase of Ecclesiasticus 50:22–24, ends with *Gloria Patri*. After the Reformation in England, hymn-singing in the Established Church was for nearly three centuries dominated by psalm paraphrases, each ending with the *Gloria*. Even the Dissenter, Watts, provided a score of doxologies in various metres for use with his hymns as well as his psalms. Wesley, however, discontinued the practice.

When hymn-singing in the Church of England was standardised by the appearance of A&M in 1861, there was a feeling among churchpeople that all hymns should at some point be addressed to God. Accordingly the compilers added a prayer or doxology to hymns whose authors had not done so. The editors of *Church Hymns*, *The Hymnal Companion* and particularly EH were for the most part faithful to original texts, but by then the A&M versions had taken root in folk-memory and to this day are regarded by some people as authentic. After the disaster of A&M 1904 (see chapter 1), one can understand the reluctance of the compilers to reform their texts. It is inconceivable, however, that the popularity of this great hymnal today owes anything to the Victorian policy of making all hymns conform to one pattern.

There is no reason why we should not sing to each other about our faith and exhort one another to live accordingly. Hymns of Teaching and Conduct, therefore, are complete in themselves. If the author has seen fit to address one of his stanzas to God it is integral; but a stanza tacked on by the editor, often unrelated in style or content, can rob the hymn of its force and individuality, and can deprive worshippers of the rich variety the Church has inherited.

PART TWO

THE MUSIC OF HYMNS

7 A GOOD TUNE

HYMNS ARE FOR SINGING. Therefore a hymn must have a tune before it can be used. Music is to a hymn as body is to soul: a soul may exist, but until it takes a body it is not said to have started life in this world. Similarly the life of a hymn does not begin until it is set to music. Blake's 'Jerusalem' had existed for over a hundred years but was unsung and virtually unknown until Parry set it to music in 1916. From that moment it came to life.

A hymn stands or falls by its tune. 'Hills of the North, rejoice', written by C.E. Oakley about 1865, appeared in the *Hymnal Companion* in 1870. But the tune there set to it lacked the distinction to match the words; consequently the hymn lay neglected until Martin Shaw composed Little Cornard for it in 1915. A recent example is 'All my hope on God is founded'. Robert Bridges wrote these verses, based on a seventeenth-century German hymn by Joachim Neander, and framed them in the same metre so as to preserve the melody which Neander himself had composed. The hymn and tune were published by Bridges in his *Yattendon Hymnal* (1899) and subsequently appeared in the collections, notably *Songs of Praise* (1933) and *The BBC Hymn Book* (1951). Neander's tune is a good example of German chorale, and Bridges's words are well matched to it; yet I cannot remember having heard the hymn sung until after it had appeared in HHT (1969) set to the tune Michael, specially composed by Herbert Howells. Here again the tune has brought the hymn to life. There must be many a fine hymn which has stayed dormant for lack of the right tune. The partnership of these 'twin-born harmonious spirits' is of paramount importance where hymns are concerned.

There are few questions on which opinions differ more than what is the best tune for a hymn. People tend to judge subjectively: 'I know what I like', they say. But those with sufficient interest and patience to read on will, I hope, begin to understand why they like what they do, and may also arrive at some standards on which to form a sound, dispassionate judgement. In attempting to answer the question of what makes a good hymn-tune, I shall work from three basic principles. First, a hymn must communicate; therefore its tune must be simple and have some common appeal. Second, if the tune is to last it must be good music of its kind. Third, the best tune is the one that gives the truest expression to the words. This last is by far the most vital criterion. No matter how good or popular a tune may be in itself, if it does not give wings to the words it fails in its purpose. For convenience, however, we shall take the other points first.

FIRST, SIMPLICITY. A melody that cannot be sung by a large body of untrained singers is of no use as a hymn-tune. This limits the compass if high and low voices are to sing it in unison with comfort. It also precludes the use of awkward intervals and complex rhythms. In the present century the radio and the development of recording have certainly familiarised the public with many new sounds; yet there are limits to what a crowd can be expected to pick up and sing effectively together.

Church music is generally a generation behind, because it is unreasonable to expect a cross-section of the public to assimilate too much that is unfamiliar all at once. Even in the concert-hall, modern music does not draw large crowds when all its dimensions—tonality, rhythm, harmony and form—are unfamiliar. If in only one of these—a wisp of memorable melody, a discernible beat, an occasional common chord, a recognisable overall shape—listeners feel at home, there is at least a foothold from which to start exploring. The greatest innovators, from Beethoven to Britten, have been mindful of this. Without a point of contact, where does communication begin?

Now if this is true in the concert-hall, where the audience is music-minded and eager to listen, how much more so in church, where the congregation is not necessarily musical and is expected to participate! There must be a point of communication. In a hymn-tune, therefore, an occasional cliché should not be despised. We shall see presently that two of our greatest sacred melodies, Goss's Praise My Soul and Parry's Jersualem, are each founded on a cliché. On hearing the opening strain of either for the first time one immediately feels at home. The skill of the composer is seen not so much in the originality of his germinal theme as in what he is able to make of it. That is why, although a hymn-tune is a humble form of art, it takes a good musician to write one.

SECOND, HYMN-TUNES AS MUSIC. However small and restricted, a hymn-tune should be judged as a work of art. The chorales of Bach are as artistically perfect as his suites and concertos. Nor is musical excellence confined to any particular period or style. Every age has produced good hymn-tunes. Some tunes of the pop genre are good music of their kind.

To test the musical quality of a tune we must begin with the melody. Ideally it should stand on its own feet without the support of harmony. Try whistling it. This will immediately show the strength of a plainsong melody like *Jesu dulcis memoria* (AMR 188) and the melodic weakness of such tunes as Pentecost (AMR 304) and St Andrew of Crete (A&M 55). (The latter, however, has saving graces, as we shall see later.) Tunes that pass the whistling test generally have either rhythm or movement.

Rhythm imparts vitality and character. Indeed, a melody can often be recognised by its rhythm alone. Take any well-known tune with a strong rhythm: say Monk's Gate (NEH 372) or Austria (A&M 172). Clap its rhythm, or tap it on the table before a group of people, and they will probably spot the melody without hearing a note. Rhythm also makes a tune memorable and hence easy to learn. It is its strong, individual rhythm that commends Sir Sydney Nicholson's Chislehurst to congregations as a stimulating alternative tune to 'Hail the day that sees him rise' (A&M 87).

There are, of course, hymns in which strong rhythmical features would be out of place. Here vitality can be imparted by movement. Plainsong has no measured rhythm, yet who can deny that it has vitality? The melody, *Jesu dulcis memoria*, is a case in point. Its vitality and beauty lie in the movement and symmetry of its phrases and their relation to one another. Notice how naturally they grow from line to line and lead finally to the restatement of the first.

A good tune is like a conversation. A statement is made,

answered and then discussed. Likewise a melody must have a starting-point, a spark of inspiration—perhaps a phrase or rhythmic figure suggested by the opening words or the mood of the hymn. From this germinal phrase the tune will grow, as a discussion grows from a chance statement. Here the composer's art begins. A good musician can make a little go a long way. Like a good conversationalist, he picks out interesting features and discusses them. This gives the tune unity.

Let us now take a look at the tunes Jerusalem (A&M 294) and Praise My Soul (A&M 192). Their words and music are now so well known and so closely associated in folk memory that the words alone should generally be sufficient to bring the music to mind.

Parry's Jerusalem springs from the germinal theme set to the words of the opening line. It is founded on a cliché, in the sense that its first four notes are the intonation of the fifth Gregorian tone. The second line begins with the last four notes of the first. Lines 3 and 4 answer the first two, carrying the argument into the dominant key. Then follows a rising sequence, again based on the germinal theme, which begins in compressed form in line 5. Note how the intervals between its first four notes grow with each entry—ray ray me fah, ray fah soh la—until in line 7 the phrase reaches its full stature, fah la doh^1 ray^1, to create a powerful climax before the final cadence (line 8) which answers the half-cadence in line 4. Thus the whole song is a unity based on a germinal theme.

Now let us look at a more typical hymn-tune: Goss's Praise My Soul. Its germinal theme, stated in the first line, is in two halves, which we shall refer to as A and B. A is four notes in monotone on soh. B is four notes of a descending scale: doh te la soh; another cliché. Compare the alleulias in *Lasst uns erfreuen* (A&M 532). The second line begins with a variation on B, starting on a lower degree of the scale—la soh fah me—but reversing the two pairs of notes thus: fah me la soh. The third line is the tonal answer to the first; the fourth starts with the inversion of B—soh la te doh. At the climactic words, 'Praise him, praise him' (or 'Alleluia') B is thundered twice, and its tonal answer brings the tune to its logical conclusion.

These two great tunes are examples of what I mean by

making a little go a long way. I do not suggest that either Parry or Goss deliberately put their melodies together like that. What I have tried to show is that, consciously or unconsciously, they have given their tunes unity.

My Scottish friends may claim Crimond as an exception. Although the first line is a promising pastoral theme offering material for development, the lines that follow do not grow from it, nor are they related to each other. They give the impression of having been composed separately. Yet the tune has achieved wide popularity in Britain and America, so much so that its name has become synonymous with Psalm 23. *Crimond* is loved because its strains are pleasing and easy to sing. Nevertheless I hope I may be forgiven for observing that it would be a sounder and, in the long run, more durable melody if it had a unifying feature.

Even a simple four-line tune should have a unifying feature. In the Old Hundredth (A&M 100) it is the three consecutive long notes at the end of each line, those in the second and fourth being inversions of those in the first and third. The third line of a tune will often correspond to the first. Sometimes the third line is identical, as in Tallis Ordinal (A&M 152), or a variation: see Dykes'; *Dominus regit me* (A&M 126). Again, the third line may be built on an inversion of the first. In Melcombe (A&M 2), for example, soh soh fah me in the first line is answered by me me fah so in the third. In Winchester New (A&M 27), the answering phrase starts with the same two notes and then carries the idea on to a higher plane. The dovetailing of phrases is a subtle and effective device. We have already seen an example in Jerusalem, where the second line begins as the first ended. The same thing happens in the sixth line of Rhosymedre (NEH 274) and in the third of Rodmell (NEH 203). And so we could go on. In a good tune there is always some relationship between the phrases, imparting that sense of inevitability which amounts to what musicians call form.

The form of a hymn-tune is generally a miniature of one or other of the two common varieties used in classical music from song to symphony. One (called binary) is in two sections: the first modulating to a relative key, the second returning to the tonic. Tallis Ordinal, cited above, is an example. The other form (called ternary) is in three sections, often known as A B A because the first and third are roughly the same, the middle section being fresh ending in the dominant key: for example, Mannheim (A&M 224). This straightforward tune, by the way, is virtually the work of Thomas Binney (1857). The chorale by Filitz, to whom it is attributed, is in a different metre, only three of its seven lines bearing any resemblance to Mannheim, which is a perfect example of ternary form.

In ternary form the first section is sometimes repeated, giving the pattern A A B A, Many Welsh melodies spring to mind: Llanfair (A&M 87/1) and St Denio (A&M 199), for instance. Such tunes are often the better for the exercise of a certain freedom by the composer within the formal pattern. The eight lines of Aberystwyth (A&M 123/2) may be itemized thus: 1, A1; 2, A2; 3, A1; 4, A3; 5, B1; 6, B2; 7, A1 inverted; 8, A1. The implicit inversion of A1 in the seventh line creates a powerful climax. Haydn does the same in Austria (A&M 172/2).

Climax forms a focal point and sense of direction. The most obvious climax is the highest melodic note on a strong beat, as in the last two examples. Occasionally, however, after a succession of high notes, the lowest note on a strong beat can produce a climactic effect, as in St Stephen (A&M 29). In Gopsal (A&M 139) Handel, having reached his highest point at the beginning of the fourth line, produces another climax by jumping down a seventh (from doh to ray) in the last line of the refrain. In Thornbury (A&M 171) Basil Harwood, having reached his highest note by step in the penultimate line, gives it renewed emphasis in the last through approaching it by leap and lengthening it to three beats. The climactic effect of the refrain, 'One Church, one faith, one Lord,' is heightened still more in the harmonised version by recourse to unison.

If the shape of the melody is such as to preclude a melodic climax at the desired point, it may be achieved harmonically. In the last bar of Innsbruck (NEH 253) Bach creates a fine climax in the tenor part. Purcell does so with his clash of parts in the penultimate bar of Westminster Abbey (A&M 332).

Contrast is always effective and can impart vitality to a long tune. The harvest hymn, 'We plough the fields', has abnormally long verses, yet there is not a dull bar in the tune. This is due to the alternate use of bold, disjunct unison and suave, conjunct harmony, and also to the change of metre for the refrain.

All these skills and devices, and more besides, are tricks of the trade which have been employed by the makers of melody. I do not claim that the examples quoted have been consciously constructed as indicated. Nor do I say that all tunes so constructed are therefore good; there are scores of published hymn-tunes bearing the marks of skilled craftsmanship which lack the divine spark and therefore get no further than the printed page. What I do claim is that a good tune has unity and vitality. Skill cannot compensate for lack of invention, but a sound technique can often aid invention.

Harmony. There are few arts in which the hand of the amateur is more surely betrayed than harmony. If he writes in the traditional style he must be well practised in the handling of chords, modulation and part-writing; if he embraces modern freedom and claims that the wrong notes are the right notes, he must know how to give them significance. In either case he needs to be a skilled artist. Harmony is so powerful an agent in the creation of accent, atmosphere and emotion that the only criterion by which it can be fairly judged is whether it achieves the desired effect. More will be said about this when we come to consider the relationship of music to words. At this stage we are concerned only with basic principles.

It is important to remember that a hymn-tune gets hard wear. As a rule every verse is sung to the same tune, often to the same harmonies. The harmony therefore must bear repetition. Experience has proved that the harmony that wears best is the simplest. A striking remark when repeated ceases to be striking. Similarly, clever or eccentric progressions, however good in themselves, will pall if used in several successive verses. For example, the harmonisation of the third verse of Praise My Soul (A&M 192) would not be suitable for the whole hymn, whereas that of verse 1 or verse 2 would. This is one reason why the chromatic harmonies favoured by Victorians are frowned upon: not that they are bad in themselves, but that they do not wear well.

Certain harmonisations by the great Bach himself will not bear repetition verse after verse. Indeed, as we shall see in chapter 9, they were not intended to do so. Look at his two setting of the Passion Chorale (NEH 90). The first, being comparatively straightforward, can be used for all verses. The alternative version was made for the place it holds in the St Matthew Passion, where it is sung once, with heartrending effect, at the moment of Christ's death. Its sensitive, chromatic progressions are appropriate to verse 4 of this hymn, as indicated, but to sing them in any other context would almost amount to sacrilege. Using EH on Palm Sunday, I have often felt that Bach's setting of *Valet will ich dir geben*, which holds a similar position in the St John Passion, is out of place when sung to the six hearty verses of 'All glory, laud and honour' (NEH 509). I am not among those who would exclude Bach's harmonisations from the hymn book. I admire EH for including so many. But it is not fair to Bach to use them indiscriminately and without regard to the text.

Recalling the three principles outlined early in this chapter, I hope that these examples have satisfied the reader on the first two: that a hymn-tune should be simple enough for a random gathering of people to pick up easily and enjoy singing together; and that, like a house or a piece of furniture, unless it is soundly constructed it will not stand the test of time. The third, on the matching of music to words, is of such paramount importance that it merits a chapter to itself.

8 THE RIGHT TUNE

'ALLELUIA' (praise the Lord). First say it in a natural voice; then declaim it; finally sing it, as one does in many Easter hymns—'Jesus lives', for example. It does not take a musician to recognise that the word gains power when it is sung.

The power thus given by music to a single word, when extended to a sentence, a line, or a stanza, provides expression. The right tune is that which the truest expression to the words. It also creates the right feeling. If the purpose of the hymn is to praise God, the tune should add lustre to the praise; if to utter a prayer, it should deepen the devotion; if to teach, it should illuminate the teaching; if to inspire, it should commend its message. Musical excellence alone does not ensure this. As our wise poet-musician, George Herbert, wrote:

> The fineness which a hymn or psalm affords
> Is when the soul unto the lines accords.

A good reader will achieve this. The right tune will enable an assembly of souls to achieve it. Music should accord to words in stress, spirit and structure.

STRESS in verse is of two kinds: metrical, determined by the rhythmic pattern of the words and measured in feet, as we saw in chapter 2; and rhetorical, demanded by the sense. Metrical stress is expressed musically by the time, which since the seventeenth century has been measured in bars. The difference between a bar and a foot, though somewhat confusing, must be borne in mind. A foot may begin or end with a strong or weak syllable, whereas the first beat of a bar is always strong and the last always weak. Thus a trochaic line, like '*Praise*, my *soul* the *King* of *heaven*', starts on a first beat, but an iambic line, like '*Awake*, my *soul*, and *with* the *sun*', starts on the last beat of the bar.

A bar may have any number of bears, though usually there are two, three or four. Bars of two or four beats are said to be in common time, those of 3 in triple. In common time the first note of each pair has a natural stress; in a four-beat bar, the first and third. In triple time only the first beat of the bar has a natural stress. This fits the dactylic line, '*Bright*est and *best* of the *sons* of the *morn*ing'; or, starting on the second beat, the anapaestic couplet:

> But of *all* thy rich *gra*ces this *grace*, Lord, im*part*:
> Take the *veil* from our *fa*ces, the *veil* from our *heart*.

When, as happens more often, a tune in triple time is set to a trochaic or iambic hymn, the syllable falling on the first beat of the bar usually occupies two beats and so is stressed by duration as well as accent, as in '*Of* the *Fa*ther's *heart* be*got*ten', or 'As *pants* the *hart* for *coo*ling *streams*'. These are examples of simple time, in which a whole note is apportioned to each beat. For the sake of completeness mention should be made of compound time, where each beat consists of a dotted note. As the dot increases the length of the note to one-and-a-half times its value, each beat may be subdivided into three half-notes or, more commonly, a whole note plus a half-note, producing the tripping rhythm of six-eight and nine-eight time often found in carols but seldom in hymns. Stainer's tune to 'There's a friend for little children' (AMR 452) is a beautiful example of a hymn in six-eight time.

As metrical stress distinguishes verse from prose it should always be observed, both in reading and singing. The time of the tune, therefore, should match the metrical rhythm of the words.

Rhetorical stress is the emphasis that a good reader will place on certain words to express feeling or to make the meaning clear. As metrical stress is generally produced rhythmically, rhetorical stress is produced by raising or lowering the pitch of the voice; this is called inflection. A group reading verse together would usually agree on the metrical rhythm but might differ as to the degree of inflection. For corporate expression, therefore, some standardisation is necessary: hence the earliest church music. Plainsong is a vocalisation of the inflections of speech. When notes began to be measured, the length of each syllable as well as its pitch was fixed. In setting verse to music, then, it is necessary to match both metre and inflection. Broadly speaking, metre is represented by time and note-values' rhetoric or feeling by the rise and fall of the melody.

Let us repeat the experiment we made at the beginning of this chapter. Read aloud a familiar first line—'Rejoice! the Lord is King'—stressing the word you consider the most important. Now sing it, first to Gopsal (A&M 139) and then to Darwall's 148th (A&M 198). Which gives the greater force to the words? Handel, who in about 1750 wrote Gopsal specially for this hymn, stresses the word 'Rejoice'; whereas Darwall's tune, though not intended for these words, stresses what is more important, the reason for rejoicing: 'the *Lord* is *King*.' This surely is the true expression of the words of this line, not only in the first verse but also in the others: 'Jesus, the Saviour, *reigns*'; 'His Kingdom cannot *fail*'; and 'He sits at God's right *hand*'.

I have already cited Gopsal as an example of sound musical construction. It is a noble tune which, after two centuries of association with this hymn, is likely to hold its place. Nevertheless, where occasion demands that the full force of these words shall be felt, I recommend Darwall's 148th.

With harmony at our disposal we have yet a third means to musical stress: the harmonic. It is not practicable here to discuss all the nuances of which harmony is capable. Suffice it to say that, basically, a change of chord will produce an accent, even though the melodic line remains uninflected. Note for example the harmonic accent on the fourth chord of Cloisters (AMR 253), and again on the chord of A flat at the beginning of the last line. A chord in its root position is stronger than an inversion; a chord approached by a leap is stronger than one approached by step.

S.S. Wesley's tune Aurelia, to 'The Church's one foundation' (A&M 170), has been criticised for its first line, the fourth chord of which is weak on two counts: it is a second inversion, and treble and tenor move to it by step while alto and bass remain static. Both the melodic inflection and the metrical accent due to its position in the bar are thus enfeebled. 'The Church's one foundation' requires a firm stress on the word 'one' and on the corresponding syllable in each verse. What was Wesley thinking about? The answer is that he was not thinking of this hymn at all. Aurelia was written for 'Jerusalem the golden', and the chord in question was doubtless weakened deliberately to modify the metrical thump—Jerus*alem*—in the first verse while leaving the chord slightly stressed for verses in which it is appropriate. Wesley was no fool: had he intended Aurelia for 'The Church's one foundation' he would probably have harmonised it differently.

NEXT, MUSIC SHOULD ACCORD WITH WORDS IN SPIRIT: that is to say, in mood or atmosphere. John Wesley's translation of the fine hymn, 'Lo, God is here, let us adore' (AMR 249), by the German mystic Tersteegen, would have been more frequently sung if set to *Mach's mit mir Gott*, with Bach's harmonies, as it now is in NEH 209.

Dykes nearly always caught the atmosphere of a hymn: his tunes to 'Holy! Holy! Holy!' and 'Eternal Father' spring to mind. With this divine gift he covered a multitude of sins. From a musical point of view *Gute Bäume bringen* (AMR 91) is a better melody than Dykes's St Andrew of Crete; but when considered in relation to the hymn 'Christian, dost thou see them' it is Dykes's tune that conveys the spirit of the words, contrasting the subtle persuasiveness of enemy agents with the bold, Christian response. Even the composer's direction to sing the fifth line of the last verse in harmony (not unison, as in the other verses) has significance: Christ is speaking to us throughout this verse.

Harmony can often be used symbolically, as in Bach's setting of *Wachet auf* (NEH 16), where the apparently lazy basses remain dormant on the first note for two-and-a-half beats and then have to run at the double to catch up with the trebles. Another example is Vaughan William's setting of *O Seigneur* to 'When morning gilds the skies' (NEH 473), where the tenors leap an octave on the word 'sings', and the basses start to chime on 'rings' in the following line.

So great is the symbolic power of music that a tune can alter the whole spirit of a hymn. Caroline Noel's 'At the name of Jesus' (A&M 148) is a case in point. The tune Evelyns, composed for it by W.H. Monk about 1875, may not be a great piece of music, but it is well-written and a serious attempt to depict Jesus as King of glory, to be named 'with awe and wonder and with bated breath'. There is no awe and wonder in the tune Camberwell, written about 1960. It puts a paper crown on his head, slaps him on the shoulder and treats him as an equal. This may reflect the current swing of emphasis from Christ as God to Christ as man; it certainly does not reflect the spirit of Caroline Noel's hymn.

FINALLY, THE OVERALL STRUCTURE of a hymn should not be overlooked when the tune is being selected. The shape of the verse can be significant. George Herbert's 'Let all the world in every corner sing' (A&M 202) is entitled 'Antiphon' and constructed accordingly. Each verse begins and ends with the chorus:

> Let all the world in every corner sing,
> My God and King!

The intervening rhyming couplets represent four sources of praise: the heavens and earth in verse 1, the Church and the human heart in verse 2. Herbert intended these lines to be sung antiphonally to produce an echo effect. Basil Harwood's tune Luckington gives appropriate musical expression to both these features.

Charles Wesley wrote 'Love divine, all loves excelling' (A&M 131) in eight-line stanzas, each working up to a climax. It is a pity that the four-line arrangement with Stainer's tune has become so popular, for it has robbed the words of much power. The eight-line Welsh tunes Blaenwern and Hyfrydol are much better suited to the emotional structure of this hymn.

A more extreme case is Bishop Mant's 'Bright the vision' (A&M 96). This six quatrains now in common use fall naturally into two cycles of twelve lines, one about the Church in heaven and the other about the Church on earth, each ending with the refrain, 'Lord, thy glory fills the heaven ...' Ideally it should have a twelve-line tune. Using Redhead's *Laus Deo*, however, the structure can still be preserved by singing the hymn in two unbroken sections, each ending with the refrain in unison or with descant.

Conversely, some four-line hymns have been incorrectly set to eight-line tunes. 'Praise the Lord! ye heavens, adore him' is particularly associated with Austria, the tune Haydn wrote during the Napoleonic wars to provide Austria with a national anthem, like the one he had heard sung with patriotic fervour when he was in London. It was called the Emperor's Hymn, and first sung before the Emperor Francis on his birthday, 12 February 1797. Later it was adopted as the German national anthem. One night in World War II, a British officer, unconsciously whistling this hymn as he strolled along the quay at one of the Channel ports, was seized and questioned by the Military Police, who thought he was a spy.

A glance at the words will reveal that 'Praise the Lord! ye heavens, adore him' consists of four quatrains, each beginning with the imperative 'Praise' and giving different grounds for it: 'Praise the Lord! ye heavens, adore him'; 'Praise the Lord! for he hath spoken'; 'Praise the Lord! for he is glorious'; and 'Praise the God of our salvation'. To sing this hymn to an eight-line tune obscures both its pattern and its message, as does also the addition by some editors of Edward Osler's doxology, 'Worship, honour, glory, blessing'. St Oswald (A&M 211), which by reason of its repetition of the first phrase is so tedious when sung to the eight verses of 'Through the night of doubt and sorrow', was actually written by Dykes for 'Praise the Lord! ye heavens, adore him' and fits its four verses admirably. The effect of the line with which each verse begins can be heightened by singing it in unison and bursting into harmony at the second line.

Poets often break monotony by varying the rhythmic pattern. Cowper, in particularly, is given to throwing in the odd trochee at the beginning of an iambic line. 'Jesus, where'er thy people meet' (A&M 162) is a case in point. Verses 1, 4 and 5 begin with a trochee and 2 and 3 with an iamb; in verses 2 and 3 it is the third line that begins with a trochee. The tune Wareham, to which this hymn is often sung, is essentially iambic: being in triple time and starting on the third beat, it gives extra stress to the second syllable of each pair, not only as falling on the first beat of the bar but also as having double duration. Thus it exaggerates the false accents in four of the five verses. A more flexible tune is Warrington (A&M 89). This also is in triple time, but its first and third lines begin on the first beat of a bar in which each beat is allotted to a syllable. In such a bar the first beat is stressed and the last unstressed, but the second beat may be stressed or unstressed as occasion demands: in this case stressed for an opening iamb, unstressed for a trochee. Warrington also suits the spirit of this hymn.

'God moves in a mysterious way' (A&M 112), also by Cowper, is another case of a fine hymn ill wedded to a fine tune. London New, with or without its gathering notes (long notes at the start of a line), creates ugly false accents by reason of its steep inflections: 'God moves in *a* myster*ious* way'; 'His purpos*es* will rip*en* fast'. Furthermore, the spirit of this tune is bold and straightforward; there is nothing mysterious about it. It is ideally suited to verse 3, but fails to match the awe and wonder of the first two verses. There are two possible solutions. One is to select a tune with less pronounced accents. Gibbons's Song 67, in its original form with a gathering note in the first line only (NEH 225), begins with the same three notes as London New but, being conjunct in movement, suits all the verses equally well. The other solution is to use two tunes, reserving London New for verses 3 and 6.

Stilted tunes like London New are hard to match to suitable words because their steep intervals commit them to strong accents. This robust and confident melody is completely at home with the hymn 'O God of truth, whose living word' (A&M 222), written by Thomas Hughes, the author of *Tom Brown's Schooldays*. To these words London New is better without gathering notes.

As the reader will have inferred, I regard the gathering notes of the old psalm-tunes as optional, depending on the mood of the hymn and the rhythm of the words. They are appropriate to hymns of devotional character, but if the spirit if one of urgency it is better to drop them. Gathering notes, however, add breadth to a melody. They can also act as a valuable counterbalance in a hymn where false accents occur. 'Let saints on earth in concert sing' (A&M 182), sung to *Dundee* without its gathering notes (as printed in A&M), has three false accents: 'Part *of* the host have crossed the flood'; 'Wait*ing* their call to rest'; 'Je*su*, be thou our constant guide'. The gathering notes (as printed in NEH 396) perform the miracle of obviating these false accents without creating new ones. The reason is that we now have a potential accent on the first as well as the second syllable: the first a note of double length, the second a strong beat. This enables the singer to stress whichever requires it.

There are, then, two ways of dealing with false accents. One is to use two tunes. 'Praise to the Holiest' raises problems to which this is probably the only practical solution. The other is to select a tune, either in common time with gathering notes or in triple time starting on the first beat of the bar, which has the same effect. Saffron Walden (NEH 294) would fit the hymn, 'Just as I am' better if the first chord of the third line were omitted altogether and the next bar began with two crotchets instead of a minim. If Rockingham were not such a beautiful, devotional melody, so close to the spirit of 'When I survey', it would have been superseded long ago because of its appalling false accents: 'Save *in* the death of Christ my God'; 'All *the* vain things that charm me most'; 'Sor*row* and love flow mingled down'; 'Spread *o'er* his body on the tree'; 'Then *am* I dead to all the globe'; 'That *were* a present far too small'. A tune in the rhythm of Maryton (AH 380) would obviate all these things; it would also enable us to sing Watt's original second line: 'Where the young Prince of glory died'.

The problem of shifting accents is undoubtedly the reason for the unadventurous rhythms of many nineteenth-century tunes. At the time when A&M first made its appearance it had become customary to write tunes in notes of uniform value. Even older melodies with strong rhythmic characteristics, such as Angel's Song (NEH 235) and Mount Ephraim, were watered down to conform to this pattern. The two versions of Mount Ephraim (AMR 531) show how drastic this could be. Thus a policy devised to avoid false accents became a rigid mould in which all tunes were cast, to the great detriment of some fine hymns.

'Breathe on me, breath of God' (A&M 157) is a valuable hymn associated with several tunes which are all in some way unsatisfactory. As the first line is the same in each verse, a tune that does not fit this line exactly can be ruled out for a start. Carlisle and Aylesbury are thus disqualified. Trentham, though not composed for this hymn, avoids the false accents but is in a style that has given Victorian hymnody a bad name. This might be forgiven if it matched the spirit of the words; if, for example, the first line had been 'O what a dreary day!' But 'Breathe on me, breath of God' is a strong prayer to the greatest force in the universe for new life, vigour, endurance and divine fire. The plaintive inflections and mawkish harmonies of Trentham give this prayer a spirit of resignation rather than confidence. Dominica (NEH 342) goes well to this hymn. A more devotional tune, however, is St Bride. As the rhythm of this melody varies in eighteenth-century tune-books I have no compunction in adapting it to suit this hymn.

The right tune can bring a hymn to life. At the beginning of chapter 7 I cited 'Hills of the North, rejoice' as an example. Martin Shaw's Little Cornard matches its rhythm as well as its atmosphere of urgency. The result is an ideal partnership: the tune owes its existence to the hymn, the hymn its popularity to the tune.

Is a new tune necessary? For a new hymn, the answer is often yes. For one already wedded to a popular tune that is good of its kind and accords with the words in every respect, no. Only when the customary tune does not do justice to the words, or has failed to catch on, or is being overworked by doing duty for several hymns, is there a good case for replacing it. In the rich heritage we already possess there are many fine tunes, unemployed, waiting for the right hymn. Failing that, there are gifted composers of our own day ready to produce a new tune, tailor-made for the words.

Changes should not be made lightly. For most people hymn and tune go together, and a mishandled attempt to break the association may lead to the loss either of the hymn or of the people concerned. Once the congregation is persuaded that the new tune gets the words across better than the old, they will accept it with enthusiasm.

I ADD A POSTSCRIPT ON DESCANTS. This exciting form of variation is much in vogue and, I fear, in danger of being overdone. A descant is more than mere decoration; it is a powerful form of musical symbolism. It can suggest fullness to overflowing: 'We'll crowd thy gates with thankful songs' (A&M 197, verse 3); 'Lord, thy glory fills the heaven' (A&M 96, verse 6). It can suggest an extra voice or voices: 'My soul, bear thou thy part' (A&M 198, verse 4); 'Angels help us to adore him (A&M 192, verse 4). It can suggest a companion: 'I need thy presence every passing hour' (A&M 13, verse 3). It can suggest bounty: 'Thou spreadst a table in my sight' (A&M 126, verse 5); 'Hail, sacred feast which Jesus makes' (A&M 259, verse 2). It can also be used to create a climax, demanded by the words but not provided by the tune, as with 'Thy kingdom stands and *grows* for ever' (A&M 16, verse 5, last two lines only). Care should always be taken to ensure that the rise and fall of the descant matches the rise and fall of the words.

9 RICH RESOURCES

A WIDE RANGE OF SOURCES, extending over a period of more than a thousand years, has produced our hymn melodies. In British and American hymnals we find not only indigenous tunes of all periods but also melodies of Swiss, French, German, Italian and Scandinavian origin. This eclecticism seems to be a peculiarity of the English-singing Church. In German hymn-books, for instance, we do not see melodies by Darwall, Dykes or Vaughan Williams. Is this because English tunes are inferior? I think not. The reasons are historical.

The short survey that follows does not claim to be a detailed history of the kind that others have already provided, most recently David Baker and Joan Welsby in *Hymns and Hymn Singing* (1993). Our prime purpose here is to display the rich variety of resources we have inherited and to trace the steps whereby English-singing Churches the world over have become eclectic where music is concerned.

WE BEGIN WITH PLAINSONG. We know from the Old Testament and other ancient writings that there was sacred music long before the Christian era; but as no manuscripts exist we do not know how it sounded. The earliest music of which we have definite knowledge is the plainsong of the Christian Church.

As may be expected, the music of over a thousand years differs from that to which our ears are accustomed. It is entirely melodic: in the heyday of plainsong, harmony was unknown. Moreover, plainsong was founded on the Greek modes, the ancestors of our major and minor scales; but whereas the latter, with their key-signatures, vary only in pitch, each of the modes has a character or mood of its own. Some idea of the effect may be obtained at the piano by playing various scales using white notes only. Thus the scale of D, on white notes, is the so-called Dorian mode; likewise E the Phrygian, F the Lydian and so on. When quoting plainsong I shall use modern notation.

Plainsong sprang from the natural rhythm and inflections

of speech. These two elements, rhythm and inflection, give life and meaning to the spoken word. We all use them consciously or unconsciously in conversation. Rhythm is imparted by the ripple of the words themselves, inflection by the expression we give them by raising or lowering the pitch of the voice as the sense demands. When a group of people wants to make a united declaration, rhythm and inflection need to be standardised so that the result is coherent. This is where music comes in.

A simple example is the first line of the Compline hymn, *Te lucis ante terminum*. The proper plainsong melody fits the Latin perfectly, as does the English translation by J.D. Chambers, which has the same rhythm and inflexions. The rhythm of this iambic line demands a slight accent on alternate syllables: 'To *thee* be*fore* the *close* of *day*'. The inflections give special emphasis to certain words as demanded by the sense: thus in speech the pitch of the voice naturally rises on the words 'thee' and 'close' and falls slightly on 'day'. Hence the plainsong:

It should be remembered that the language of plainsong is Latin. It is not easy for the translator to achieve a perfect match in inflection as well as meaning and rhythm. Even the familiar English version of this line—by J.M. Neale, whose ear was usually sensitive to melody—produces the glaring false accent, 'Before the ending *of* the day'. The translator's problem is further illustrated by the opening of the famous Passiontide hymn,

> *Pange lingua gloriosi*
> *proelium certaminis.*

'Sing, my tongue, the glorious battle' conveys the sense and spirit of the Latin, but misses the point of the triumphant lilt given by the proper melody to the word *gloriosi*:

Pan - ge lin - gua glo - ri - o - - si

Feeling is often expressed in speech by change of pitch during the articulation of one syllable, as here. The plainsong equivalent is a group of two or more notes, known as a neum. Further examples are to be found in the other Passiontide hymn, *Vexilla regis prodeunt*, by the same author. Here Neale's translation matches the Latin well: 'The royal banners forward go'. In uttering these words the voice naturally slides up on the first syllable of 'royal', down and up a little on 'banners', and so on. This is precisely the contour of the melody.

The roy - al ban - ners for - ward go.

How well this flowing tune suggests the flying of flags! A florid outburst of notes on a single syllable, called melisma, creates a melodic climax while adding lustre to the syllable it adorns. There is one in the fourth line of this tune; Neale has been careful to give it a suitable word in each verse, particularly the third (NEH 79):

Hath reigned and tri - - umph'd from the tree.

It is perhaps too much to expect the same tune to match all the verses equally well, but the principles of plainsong are basic to the setting of words to music of any kind. Generally the proper speed of plainsong is that of speech.

Plainsong does not lend itself to full-throated, hearty singing, and therefore is unlikely to achieve the wide popularity of later tunes with a measured rhythm and emotional climax. The fact remains that as a vehicle for the words to which it was set plainsong is unsurpassed. It has an important role in modern worship by reason of its age-long association with certain hymns to which, even in translation, it is still appropriate. Now that the ear of the public has been emancipated from the diatonic scale, the time is ripe for the revival of plainsong, not to the exclusion of all else, but to take its rightful place in the rich and varied heritage of church music.

THE LATTER MIDDLE AGES saw the decline of plainsong in its purest form. Partly through use in procession and partly through the development of harmony, hymn melodies were hammered into a measured beat. As most of the old Latin hymns were written in iambic or trochaic metres, it is not surprising that the earliest fixed rhythm consisted of alternate two- and one-pulse notes now known as triple time:

This is the first line of a tune still in common use. It is said to be the work of Pierre de Corbeil, a twelfth-century French priest; he held appointments in England, notably as Archdeacon of York, and became Archbishop of Sens. The tune was associated with the Feast of the Ass, a popular French festival on 14 January, commemorating the flight of the Holy Family to Egypt. The procession to the church was headed by a richly bedizened donkey on which were seated a girl and babe in arms. On the way the people chanted a hymn beginning *Orientis partibus adventavit assinus* to this tune, with the refrain *Hez sire assnez, hez*—'Hail, sir donkey, hail!' Contemporary manuscripts differ. Thirteenth-century notation is not clear as to the rhythm, but it is hard to imagine the villagers in procession chanting these words in anything but triple time.

From then until the Reformation the popularity of processions and dancing in connection with religious festivals must have given considerable impetus to measured singing. Moreover, the invention of printing in the fifteenth century made possible a more uniform method of notation. To this period belong many of the lovely, lilting modal carols revived by G.R. Woodward in *The Cowley Carol Book* (1902).

The Swedish collection, *Piae Cantiones* (1582), is a treasury of such tunes. One in particular, now sung to the Christmas processional 'Of the Father's heart begotten', is typical of the beating of plainsong into measured music between the thirteenth and sixteenth centuries. The plainsong melody appeared in an early manuscript as a trope to the *Sanctus*, beginning:

Di - vi - num mys - ter - i - um Sem - per de - cla - ra - - tur.

Later manuscripts of this trope give different versions of the tune. In *Piae Cantiones* it is printed in triple time as we sing it today. The English words of our Christmas hymn, written to carry this tune, are a translation of selected stanzas from a Latin poem by Prudentius entitled 'Miracles of Christ'.

In France during the sixteenth century plainsong melodies gave place to measured tunes: some in triple time like the donkey tune, some in sapphic metre. Many are thought to have been founded on plainsong, others on secular tunes. Some two dozen of these melodies were introduced to Anglican worshippers by EH (1906): 18, 141 and 335, for example. They have a joyous solemnity, well preserved by Vaughan William's harmonisation in that book. One in particular, *Deus tuorum militum*, has in my opinion been robbed of much dignity recently by being reharmonised and sung too fast.

GERMAN HYMNODY shows the same pattern. Martin Luther (1483–1546), who was far less puritan than Calvin and other Reformers, launched the Reformation with song. Besides his own compositions and those of his contemporaries he drew upon pre-Reformation hymns in translation; with his musical colleagues, notably Johann Walther, he adapted and harmonised their plainsong melodies: *Allein Gott* (A&M 387) for example. The word 'chorale', now associated with German hymn-tunes of the Reformation, originally referred to plainsong sung by all, as distinct from solo passages.

Between 1524 and his death Luther and the poets and musicians he gathered round him produced several collections of hymns. A number of these hymns and some of the tunes are attributed to Luther himself, but without certainty. About one at least there is no doubt. Luther wrote the words of *Ein' feste Burg*, based on the opening sentence of psalm 46; he also wrote the tune, which began thus:

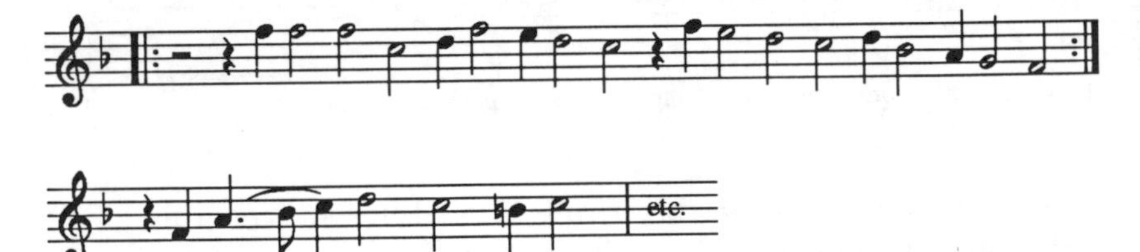

The irregularity of rhythm which characterizes church melodies of that period may be an unconscious combination of the unbarred speech-rhythm of plainsong with the new music of the day. In the first line, given here, one can sense the lingering flavour of plainsong despite its harmonic structure; whereas the phrase at the beginning of the next line reminds one of a madrigal.

'Why should the Devil have all the best tunes?' asked Rowland Hill in the nineteenth century. It seems that Luther and his successors had similar sentiments. The much-loved tune we call *Innsbruck* (NEH 253) was composed about 1500 by Heinrich Isaac for the song of a homesick traveller: 'Innsbruck, I now must leave thee'. Inspired by this song a generation later, Johann Hesse wrote 'O world, I now must leave thee'—a hymn for criminals sentenced to death—to fit the same melody, which thus found its way into church. Later it was attached to the words by Paul Gerhardt on which Robert Bridges based his evening hymn, 'The duteous day now closeth'.

Even the solemn melody of the passion chorale 'O sacred head' (A&M 68) was originally a love song: 'My heart is distracted by a pretty maid', or words to that effect. Its composer, Hans Leo Hassler, a prominent musician of his day, died a year before it was included in *Harmoniae Sacrae* (1613) as the tune to a German translation of the medieval Latin hymn *Salve caput cruentatum*, of which 'O sacred head' is the English equivalent.

After Luther's death the corpus of German hymnody continued to grow, the outstanding melodist of the period being Johann Crüger (1598–1662). As cantor of the Lutheran cathedral of St Nicholas, Berlin, for the last forty years of his life he founded its choir and made it famous. Of his many tunes the best known in England are those inseparably associated with these hymns: 'Deck thyself, my soul, with gladness'—*Schmücke dich* (A&M 257); 'Ah, holy Jesu, how hast thou offended?'—*Herzliebster Jesu* (NEH 62); 'Hail to the Lord's anointed'—*Crüger* (A&M 142); 'Now thank we all our God'—*Nun danket* (A&M 205). *Schmücke dich* is now sung as Crüger wrote it, with syncopated rhythm in the fifth and sixth lines. The other three tunes have been altered. *Herzliebster Jesu* is known to us from Bach's settings in the St Matthew Passion. The tune called *Crüger*, which we sing to 'Hail to the Lord's anointed', had been radically altered in Germany before W. H. Monk gave it a new look for A&M in 1861. Though bearing little resemblance to what Crüger wrote in 1640, it carries the words to this English hymn with the ring of inevitability. Our version of *Nun danket* is based on the setting of it by Mendelssohn in his 'Hymn of Praise'. Crüger's original melody is as follows:

Many of the alterations had already been made before Mendelssohn came on the scene; but as far as I can discover he is responsible for the change in the contour of lines 5 and 6, a change surely for the worse, for it robs the climax in the seventh line of its effect. Mendelsson, however, was too fine an artist to fall into this trap. The effect is right in 'Hymn of Praise', where the first verse is sung unaccompanied in six-part harmony and the next in unison with an exciting figured accompaniment. Our four-part arrangement of it as a hymn tune is another matter. The restoration of Crüger's version of the last four lines would give the melody a better climax, break the rhythmic monotony of these lines and match the English words of Rinkart's hymn, 'Now thank we all our God'.

Between the death of Luther (1546) and the birth of Bach (1685) there took place three developments which made congregational participation in the singing of chorales easier. First came the transference of the melody from tenor to treble, causing it to stand out more clearly. This is the arrangement in Lucas Ossiander's *Fifty Sacred Songs and Psalms* (1586); but whereas Ossiander, a priest, saw in it an aid to congregational singing, the reason why it was adopted by such musicians as Vulpius and Praetorius is more likely to have been the trend of German music at that time towards the melodic Italian style. Secondly, in the mid-seventeenth century the organ took the place of the choir in leading the singing. This was made possible by progress in organ-building. Thirdly, the irregular rhythms of the old melodies were replaced by notes of uniform value. For example *Nun danket alle Gott*, of which we have already seen Crüger's original version, had been given its present four-square rhythm by the end of the seventeenth-century, though the notes themselves were as yet unchanged.

Many old melodies have been considerably altered over the years. It is interesting to compare Paderborn (A&M 149) with Daily Daily (NEH 188). In style and rhythm they are very different. On closer inspection, however, they will be found to be alike in contour and chord-sequence. Indeed they could be the German and French descendants, respectively, of the same melody—perhaps a Tyrolese folk-song.

Most of the German tunes sung in England are chorales. We have, however, two of Catholic origin: the well-known *Lasst uns erfreuen* (A&M 532), and *Ave virgo virginum*. The version of the latter given in A&M 443 is the earliest and the best. With it syncopated sixth line it goes well to the Easter hymn, 'Come, ye faithful, raise the strain'.

CONSIDERING JOHANN SEBASTIAN BACH'S life-work in the service of the Church, his output of original hymns was small. He was essentially a practical musician, writing and arranging music on demand. New hymns were seldom required, but there was scope for the harmonisation of the traditional melodies, shorn as they had been of their rhythmic features.

When Bach as a choirboy sang the chorale *Ein 'feste Burg*, it probably took the form of A below. Compare this with Luther's original first line quoted on page 150. Then compare Bach's own version—B below. Both versions are printed in *A&M Old Standard Edition*, 378.

It will be noted that Bach uses the version he learnt as a boy, adding passing notes and elaborating the lower parts, each of which becomes a melody in itself. The tune loses nothing of its monolithic grandeur as it glides through the waves of harmony with the dignity of a dreadnought.

In his cantatas and passions, Bach made free use of the popular chorale melodies to symbolize the voice of the

Church, varying his harmonies to suit the text. Some 400 such arrangements have been collected, many of the melodies having been set in a variety of ways: there are nine different harmonisations of the Passion Chorale, and so on. Bach is always sensitive to words, as is shown in his four different settings of the same melody in the St Matthew Passion—from no. 23, 'Here would I stand beside thee', in which the Church echoes Peter's self-confidence at the Last Supper, to no. 72, the prayer at the foot of the cross, 'Be near me, Lord, when dying'. Or compare the rhapsodical 'Jesu, joy of man's desiring' with the devotional treatment of the same melody in St Matthew Passion no. 48, 'Lamb of God, I fall before thee'. In the former, Schope's tune is decked in scintillating festal attire; in the latter it wears, if not a hair shirt, at least a purple cope.

METRICAL PSALM-TUNES come next. While Luther in Germany was launching the Reformation with song, the Swiss Reformers were adopting a more puritan line. Zwingli and Calvin limited singing in worship to that of Bible words, mostly Psalms. So when English Protestants took refuge in Geneva during the reign of Queen Mary (1553–1558) they found Clement Marot busily preparing a French metrical psalter, and Louis Bourgeois and Claude Goudimel composing or arranging the music. The result is known as the *Genevan Psalter*.

Work on an English psalter had already been begun by Thomas Sternhold, and continued after his death by John Hopkins, before the exile. A selection of some of the fifty psalm paraphrases, including some by William Whittingham, was printed in 1556 for the use of the English congregation in Geneva. Two further editions followed in 1558 and 1561 with additional paraphrases by William Kethe and a number of tunes from the *Genevan Psalter*, which the English had learnt and liked. On returning to this country the exiles brought these 'Genevan' tunes (they were really French) with them. One was the melody set in the *Genevan Psalter* to Psalm 134, which the English wedded to Kethe's paraphrase of Psalm 100, 'All people that on earth do well' (A&M 100). This long and happy marriage has given the famous tune its English name, Old Hundredth. We sing this melody today as Bourgeois wrote it, except the last line, which originally began with three long notes, giving the melody greater strength and breaking the monotony of four lines in the same rhythm. Now that adventurous rhythms in church music are fashionable, the restoration of this fine tune to its original form is overdue.

Genevan psalm tunes, like German chorales, were often irregular in rhythm and suffered much adaptation in succeeding years. Bach wrote three settings of the *Old Hundredth* in triple time.

Among other tunes from the *Genevan Psalter* are: *O Seigneur* (Psalm 3), set to 'When morning gilds the skies' (NEH 473), to which it is well suited; *Rendez à Dieu* (Psalm 118), now associated with Heber's communion hymn 'Bread of the world in mercy broken' (A&M 270/1); *Les dix commandements*, debased to fit the LM of Whittingham's paraphrase of the ten commandments, but in A&M 270/2 given in its original form; and the Old 124th, of which the slightly adapted English version, now associated with Clifford Bax's words 'Turn back, O man, forswear thy foolish ways', first appeared in Day's Psalter 1562. Gustav Holst has written a fine arrangement of it.

The first complete English Psalter (1562) was printed in London by John Day, a keen Protestant and enterprising printer with a flair for self-advertisement. His emblem was a sleeper aroused by a man pointing to the rising sun, with the motto 'Arise for it is Day'. This book, containing all the Psalms and certain other Prayer Book passages versified by Sternhold, Hopkins and others, is generally designated the *Old Version*. It was the standard psalter authorised for use in the Church of England until the *New Version* of Brady and Tate appeared in 1696. Meanwhile the words, crude and unadventurous as they were, remained unaltered. But there were important improvements to the music. The fist edition had only 47 tunes, melody only. Among them were a round dozen from the *Genevan Psalter* (which had lost much of their character through being forced to fit English metres), *Vater unser* from *Geistliche Lieder* 1539, and anonymous English melodies, some adapted from plainsong. They are nearly all in DCM and amount to littel more than strings of unrelated phrases. An exception is the Old 81st (AMR 529), which has more shape. It is possible to see in these crude originals the seeds from which the modern English hymn-tune grew. In time these DCM tunes were replaced by more compact four-line versions. The tune we now call St Flavian is the first half of an old DCM tune. In the second edition (1563) more tunes were added, and all were harmonised for four voices—the melody in the tenor—by Parsons, Causton and others.

Damon's Psalter (1579) consisted mainly of reharmonisations. One of the few new melodies was *Southwell* (A&M 129/2, NEH 70). But Damon, organist of the Chapel Royal, was dissatisfied and withdrew the book. In 1591 he published a much more elaborate edition 'for the recreation of such as delight in music'. Hence the tune was placed in the highest part, instead of the tenor, for the first time in England.

Thomas Este (East) was a printer and publisher. His psalter of 1592, the first in which the tunes are given names, is important for its harmonisations, which were done by notable musicians of the day, including John Dowland and Giles Farnaby, and for the first appearance of Winchester Old, the tune now sung to 'While Shepherds watched'. Richard Allison, who also contributed to Este's Psalter, published his own psalter in 1599, printed after the manner of madrigals so that, sitting round a table, singers and instrumentalists could use the same book.

Thomas Ravenscroft's Psalter (1621) furthered the system of naming tunes. Musically this is the richest of all editions of the *Old Version*. Harmonisations by leading contemporary musicians are included, with many by Ravenscroft himself. Several fine tunes make their first appearance, notably Lincoln (NEH 126) and Old 104th (A&M 298, NEH 216). In the second line of Lincoln the second note was doubled—not the first as in the other lines: the restoration of this rhythm would suit most CM verses. As for the Old 104th, there was a great lengthening of notes in the last of its four lines. These have long since been removed, so robbing it of the rhythmic climax the composer intended. *The Church*

Hymnary (1927) doubled the last four notes, no doubt to stress the refrain. *The Hymn Book of the Church of Canada* (1971) added the original last line with simplified harmonics as an alternative. Surely the simplest way to achieve a climax here would be to halve the last note of line 3 and double the first of line 4, so stressing the second beat of the bar.

The Scottish Psalter of 1564 was much richer in music than the corresponding English one. It included more French tunes from the *Genevan Psalter*, with German chorales and British melodies in a greater variety of metres. Many of these proved too difficult for country congregations; in subsequent editions greater simplicity was sought. One innovation of lasting importance was the introduction in 1615 of a number of four-line tunes suitable to any words in CM. Some of them are now in use throughout the English-singing world. Their names will strike a familiar chord with most choristers: Dundee, Dunfermline and York (1615), Caithness and London New (1635).

Thomas Tallis, by far the greatest composer of his generation, wrote nine modal tunes for Matthew Parker's Psalter in 1567; but as Parker's Psalter was not adopted officially, these tunes had to wait for recognition. Among them are the famous Canon (A&M 10)—originally in DCM, with each line repeated—and the Ordinal (A&M 152). These are in the Ionian mode, which is the same as our major scale. Of the other seven, four are in EH. They are exquisite pieces of music, especially Third Mode Melody (NEH 373), on which Vaughan Williams founded his Fantasia; but they need a good choir to do them justice, and have not won general acceptance as hymn-tunes.

The tunes of the *Old Version*, having once become established, were hard to dislodge; and so it was that the distinguished musicians who gathered around the Chapel Royal in the last quarter of the sixteenth century contented themselves with harmonising and arranging them. Early in the seventeenth century, two notable composers wrote hymn-tunes. One was Orlando Gibbons, who in 1623 contributed seventeen tunes to George Wither's *Hymns and Songs of the Church*. All of them are very simple and of great beauty; at least two, Song 1 and Song 34 are among the best known hymn-tunes in use today. (Gibbons wrote three versions of Song 34: the LM tune known as Angel's Song; Song 9, the same with two extra lines; and Song 44, with the two extra lines repeated. The rhythm of the first line in NEH 235 is that of Song 9. A&M 239 gives that of Song 34. The use of two versions for the same words is confusing to church-people. To Gibbons it depended on the words he was setting.) The other composer was Henry Lawes, who wrote some fine tunes for Sandy's *Psalm Paraphrases* of 1638. A well known example is Farley Castle (A&M 62). In Gibbons and Lawes England had at last produced composers in the field of hymnody who were a match for Louis Bourgeois.

THE RESTORATION was not an instant process. From the devastation of its music by the Commonwealth regime, 1649–1660, the Church took a long time to recover. The most significant effort to restore congregational singing was made by John Playford, who in 1648 had founded a music publishing firm in London. His was the first psalter after the Restoration, entitled *Psalms and Hymns in Solemn Music* (1671). It was an elaborate volume, remarkable for the fact that it contained some paraphrases not in the *Old Version* and also a handful of hymns. Most of the forty-seven tunes had already appeared in Ravenscroft and other psalters, but all were reset for men's voices. At the end was a *Gloria Patri* by Benjamin Rogers. This book was not accepted, and in 1677 Playford issued a much simpler volume entitled *The Whole Book of Psalms*. This became the standard setting of the *Old Version*. John Playford was responsible for the introduction of the tunes St Mary (A&M 222/1, NEH 402) from Pry's Welsh Psalter, and *London New* (A&M 112, NEH 365) from the Scottish Psalter, as also for giving them their present forms. When he died an elegy to him by Nahum Tate (author of 'While shepherds watched') was set to music by Henry Purcell. Under the direction of John's son, Henry, the firm of Playford continued to publish music well into the eighteenth century.

Henry Purcell (1659–1695), one of the most gifted English composers of all time, was not required to write any psalm or hymn-tunes. The only one bearing his name, Westminster

Abbey (A&M 332), is an adaptation of a hallelujah chorus at the end of his anthem 'O God, thou art my God'.

THE START OF THE EIGHTEENTH CENTURY marked a turning-point in English hymnody. We have already noted the unsuccessful attempts of George Wither, Playford and others to introduce hymns, as distinct from psalm paraphrases into the church service. The *New Version* of the psalms, by Nahum Tate and Nicholas Brady, appeared in 1696, and in 1700 a Supplement: in addition to the customary Creed, Lord's Prayer, Ten Commandments, and so on, it provided six new hymns, including 'While shepherds watched'. More hymns were added in later editions. In 1701 appeared Playford's *Divine Companion or David's Harp New Tuned*, followed by a second and enlarged edition in 1709. Then came Isaac Watts, the Independent, who wrote 600 hymns, and a generation later Charles Wesley, with his 6000 hymns. The monopoly of the metrical psalter was at an end.

The music composed for this vast output of hymnody is in three styles. First is the school of Purcell, which is merely a heading of convenience. There is no composer like Purcell. At the turn of the century there flourished in this country a handful of operatic and song composers who were clearly influenced by him. Two such men were William Croft (1678–1727) and Jeremiah Clarke (c. 1670–1707). Croft became organist of Westminster Abbey in 1708, and thenceforth devoted all his energies to church music. Two famous tunes, St Anne (now inseparable from 'O God our help') and Hanover ('O worship the King') are almost certainly by him. They first appeared in the sixth edition of *A Supplement to the New Version* (1708), set to Psalms 42 and 67 respectively. Among Croft's other tunes are St Matthew (A&M 285), Binchester (A&M 176), and Croft's 136th (A&M 316). Jeremiah Clarke, composer of the well-known Trumpet Voluntary (for many years attributed to Purcell), like Croft sang as a boy in the choir of the Chapel Royal under Blow. In 1695 he became organist of St Paul's Cathedral. His music is more expressive and emotional than Croft's, as shown in his hymn tunes: St Magnus (A&M 141), Brockham (A&M 429), Tunbridge (NEH 481), Uffingham

(A&M 183). The early end to Clarke's promising career was tragic. There is a story—told by Bumpus in *A History of Cathedral Music* (1908) and quoted by Kenneth Long in The *Music of the English Church* (1971)—that, having been crossed in love, Clarke resolved to end his life. He rode into the country and, coming to a pond with trees near it, debated whether to drown or hang himself. He tossed up, but the coin fell edgeways in the clay. Thereupon he rode home and shot himself.

Second come minuet tunes. They are not, of course, minuets in the true sense; only in time and style do they remind one of this stately dance, which reached the peak of its popularity in the mid-eighteenth century. The tune Surrey (A&M 111) is typical. Its composer, Henry Carey, wrote the poem 'Sally in our alley' and set it to music, though not the tune we know. Surrey was written in 1723 for Addison's paraphrase of Psalm 23, the grace notes being added soon afterwards when ornament became fashionable. Most of the tunes in this style are four-liners, of which the following are well known examples: Abridge, Bishopthorpe, Irish, Manchester, Richmond, Rockingham, Wareham, Warrington and Wiltshire. Others, like Carlisle and University, though not in triple time, are akin to the minuet tunes in style and feeling. (Compare the third lines of *Carlisle* and *Richmond*.)

Third is the music of Methodism. At this time Handel was in England, and a Hanoverian monarch on the throne. Thus English musical life was dominated by foreign influence until the end of the nineteenth century. The Wesley brothers imported several tunes from Germany, doubtless as a result of their visit to the Moravian settlement at Herrnhut. One, Savannah, appeared in the Foundery collection of 1742. Like Luther two centuries earlier, John Wesley was determined to get people singing about their faith. Though his zeal exceeded his musical taste, it cannot be denied that he was successful. Many tunes associated with the Methodist revival are in the highly ornamental secular style of that time. Vocal exuberance often took precedence over suitability to the words. Their use of imitation (a debased form of that introduced by Tye in his *Acts of the Apostles*) and melisma (a florid outburst on a single syllable), after the fashion of Handel's fugal choruses, earned them the nickname 'fuguing tunes'. One, Lyngham, printed in the Methodist Hymn-book of 1933 (Appendix 10), is still sung to 'O for a thousand tongues to sing'. A few tunes in this style (though not real fuguing tunes) are as imperishable as the words to which they have been sung for well over two centuries.

'Jesus Christ is risen today', words (verse 1 only) and music, appeared anonymously as early as 1708 in *Lyra Davidica*. Later two verses were added and the tune took its present form. Compare the two versions in EH 133. The tune Helmsley was written for 'Lo! he comes', by Thomas Oliver, author of 'The God of Abraham praise', and was included in Wesley's *Select Hymns* (second edition, 1765). The tune of 'O come, all ye faithful', like its Latin words, is probably of Roman Catholic origin. On internal evidence it cannot be earlier than the eighteenth century. Each of these three tunes was written or adapted expressly for the words. This, as well as their intrinsic merit, accounts for their survival. In the first the melisma is on 'Alleluia', which raised no problems; in 'Lo! he comes' the words that have to be repeated happen to be appropriate in every verse; in 'O come, all ye faithful' the repetition of the phrase, 'O come, let us adore him' in the refrain is the making of the hymn. Indeed, the most successful use of this type of tune is to hymns with refrains. The tune Miles Lane by William Shrubsole is ideally suited to 'All hail the power of Jesu's name'. It is the only known composition by Shrubsole, who was for a time organist of Bangor Cathedral, but was dismissed for his sympathy with Dissenters and became organist of Spa Fields Chapel. The restoration of Shrubsole's second line, which ended on doh, is desirable.

The indiscriminate use of tunes which require the repetition of part of a line, when the words are different in each verse, can lead to trouble sooner or later, as is shown in the these examples from Watts: 'Take off his clothes, Take off his clothes, Take off his clothes of shame and sin'; 'Our foes of victory dream in vain And wear the cap, And wear the cap, And wear the captivating chain'; 'For God, the gracious and the good, Receives the fee, Receives the fee, Receives the feeble and the strong'.

The Welsh tune Cwm Rhondda, written by John Hughes as recently as 1905, is a highly successful modern example of this genre. It is interesting to note that Handel, whose operatic style was so much imitated and vulgarised in fuguing tunes, set a very different example in the three hymn-tunes he wrote for Charles Wesley. The best known is Gopsal to 'Rejoice, the Lord is King'.

By permission of the Syndics of the Fitzwilliam Museum

UNTIL THE ACCESSION OF QUEEN VICTORIA in 1837 there was little change in the ambience of public worship. As far as hymns were concerned, fuguing tunes continued to be popular in Nonconformist circles; and some new tunes appeared, such as Stockton (A&M 230), Crediton (A&M 502) and Martyrdom (A&M 216), in a more sober eighteenth-century style, which is but one step removed from the later psalm tunes and one step behind the early Victorians.

During these twilight years two events took place which were to have far reaching effects. First, in 1821 hymns were made legal in the Church of England. This enabled Anglicans to follow up the lead given in the preceding century by Nonconformists. Second, Keble's Assize sermon in 1833 launched the Oxford Movement. One effect of its revival of interest in medieval forms of piety was the translation of Latin and Greek hymns into singable English by John Mason Neale. If this warm-hearted scholar-poet had lived three centuries earlier to co-operate with Cranmer in producing a hymnal companion to the Book of Common Prayer, how different things might have been! Another result of the Oxford Movement was the establishment of the robed chancel choir in place of the west-end gallery choir.

The scene was thus set for the spate of hymns which inundated the Church from 1840 onwards. The tunes, hardly fewer, fall into two classes. On the whole the older men like Goss, Gauntlett, Wesley, Ouseley and Monk wrote in a style very little removed from that of Stockton and Martyrdom. But in Dykes and his successors a new quality appeared. England was by then under the spell of the Romantic movement; Mendelssohn had been a frequent visitor, and his part-songs enjoyed great popularity. His influence, with that of Spohr and Gounod, can be seen in the church music of the later Victorians—not least in their hymn-tunes.

Sir John Goss (1800–1880), wrote much church music but few hymn-tunes. Nevertheless he has the distinction of having composed, in my opinion, the finest hymn-tune of the century: Praise, My Soul (analysed in chapter 7).

Henry John Gauntlett (1805–1876) gave up the legal profession at the age of 39 and devoted himself to music. He is said to have written several thousand hymn-tunes. With all that practice it would be strange if he had not produced some good ones. There are nine in A&M, six in NEH and nine in AH. His tunes to 'Once in royal David's city' and 'Jesus lives' are known throughout the English-speaking world.

Henry Smart (1813–1879), another lawyer turned musician, became a noted organist and composer. His hymn-tunes are well constructed and often characterised by a strong, marching quality: Heathlands (A&M 179), Regent Square (A&M 185).

George Job Elvey (1816–1893) wrote the well-known tunes to 'Come, ye thankful people, come' and 'Crown him with many crowns'. His tune Pilgrimage to 'Guide me, O thou great Redeemer' is notable in that it avoids repeating the words of the fifth line.

Samuel Sebastian Wesley (1810–1876), son of Samuel Wesley the musician and grandson of Charles the hymn-writer, was the greatest English church composer in the nineteenth century before Stanford. His hymn-tunes, like everything else he wrote, bear the stamp of his genius. Not only had he the gift of writing singable melodies often of great beauty, like Hereford (A&M 233), but also of clothing them in harmonic idioms of his own. Note, for example, his use of suspensions in Cornwall (A&M 124), and the contrary motion in Colchester (A&M 243), where he does not flinch from the discord caused by the continued descent of the bass at the beginning of the last line. His tune Gweedore to his grandfather's hymn, 'Author of life divine' (A&M 258), has a striking modulation in the fourth line, characteristic of his anthems. Before leaving Wesley, let me put in a word for Hornsea to 'On the resurrection morning', relegated by EH to the Appendix (28) in the purge of 1933, ignored by AH, and abolished with the hymn by A&M in 1950. It is a little gem embodying many characteristic touches.

Richard Redhead (1820–1901) was an enthusiastic supporter of the Oxford Movement. While organist of Margaret Chapel in London (now All Saints', Margaret Street), he made several collections of hymns with tunes composed or arranged by himself. The famous tune to 'Rock of ages' is his; so is St Prisca (AMR 105), which is similar. The excellent tune now belonging to 'Bright the vision' (A&M 96), at one time thought to be of German origin, is almost certainly Redhead's own. Perhaps his best is the tune bearing the intriguing name Metzler's Redhead (A&M

86, NEH 129). Metzler was the name of Redhead's publisher.

William Henry Monk (1823–1889) has influenced English hymnody more than most, partly on account of his position as musical editor of A&M (it was he who suggested the title *Hymns Ancient & Modern*) and partly because of his approach to the task. What has been termed 'the Procrustean bed of the Victorian hymn-tune' was largely of his making. On the one hand he eschewed the rhythms and grace notes of the previous century; on the other, though certainly a Romantic, he generally managed to keep a stiff upper lip. The style he crystallised had become accepted in the second quarter of the century: square in rhythm, and harmonised according to the textbook, like psalm tunes without the gathering note. This symbolised the respectable conventions of an age when peculiarities were regarded as vulgar. Within these limits Monk contributed some melodies of lasting value. In Merton (A&M 24) he strikes the Advent note by reminding us of the first line of *Wachet auf*. St Ethelwald (A&M 219) and Evelyns (A&M 148) are also typical of Monk's style. His famous tune to 'Abide with me' (A&M 13) shows more emotion than usual, but its descent from Genevan psalmody is discernible. Compare the Old 124th (A&M 206).

Given a good opening phrase, Monk could construct a tune with the ring of inevitability. This facility led him to rewrite old melodies to make them 'respectable'. The foreign he Anglicised; the English he Victorianised. The tunes to 'Hail to the Lord's anointed', 'Lord, thy word abideth', 'Christ the Lord is risen again' and 'The strife is o'er' (Palestrina, my foot!) would probably never have been popular without their Monk's habit.

Edwin George Monk, four years his senior, who wrote Angel Voices (A&M 163), was no relation.

Sir Frederick Gore Ouseley (1825–1889) founder of St Michael's College, Tenbury, collaborated with W.H. Monk in the production of A&M. He was a scholarly musician and could write effectively in any style he chose. His Lenten tune Hereford (AMR 88; the other tune of that name besides S.S. Wesley's) is in the style of a psalm tune; Contemplation

(A&M 109) is in eighteenth-century idiom; St Gabriel (AMR 19) is Victorian.

John Bacchus Dykes (1823–1876) is the most praised and most criticised of all hymn-composers. Now that we are past the centenary of his death, the time is ripe for a brief appraisal of his work. It is important to remember that Dykes was first a priest and second a musician. His happiest years were spent as precentor of Durham Cathedral. Then in 1862 he was presented by the Dean and Chapter to the living of St Oswald's, Durham. It was an ill-judged appointment, for Dykes had distinctly high-church sympathies and St Oswald's had previously been low-church The Bishop refused to license a curate to him, and Dykes died of frustration and overwork at the age of 52.

He was the earliest exponent of a new style of hymn-tune which dramatised the emotional content of the words. He wrote 276 tunes. In such an output strengths and weaknesses are bound to show. To take the latter first, at time he seems unable to sustain the inspiration of his opening bars. St Drostane (A&M 61), for example, crumbles after the first two lines. Even the popular *Lux benigna* (A&M 215) becomes laboured towards the end. Another fault is to set the words of the first verse without apparently looking any further. St Cuthbert (A&M 151) so sentimentalises our Lord's 'tender, last farewell' that we are apt to forget that the subject of the hymn is the invigorating power of the Holy Spirit. Gerontius (A&M 117) is admirably suited to the first and last verses of 'Praise to the holiest', but less so to the others, particularly the sixth.

Nevertheless it is significant that several hymns are inseparable from the tunes Dykes wrote for them well over a century ago: 'Holy, Holy, Holy' (Nicaea); 'The King of love' (*Dominus regit me*); 'Eternal Father' (Melita); 'Fierce raged the tempest' (St Aelred); 'O strength and stay' (Strength and Stay); 'Hark, my soul' (St Bees); 'Nearer, my God, to thee' (Horbury); 'O come and mourn' (St Cross); 'I heard the voice of Jesus say' (*Vox dilecti*); 'Christian, dost thou see them' (St Andrew of Crete); 'Father of heaven' (Rivaulx); 'Ten thousand times ten thousand' (Alford).

In chapter 8 we noted Dykes's genius for capturing the atmosphere of a hymn and expressing it in music. This is his greatest strength: it accounts for the lasting association of his tunes with those hymns. The tunes were tailor-made for the words, which they match in stress, spirit and structure. It is therefore a mistake to set them to other hymns. St Oswald, as we have seen, was written for 'Praise the Lord, ye heavens adore him', and ought never to have been set to 'Through the night of doubt and sorrow'. I am convinced that Dykes conceived his tunes as a whole—melody and harmony—in relation to the words. This is the only way to judge them fairly. Alter one note of the harmony and the tune loses its character. Compare the original version of Strength and Stay, as given in the Old Standard edition of A&M (12), with the expurgated version in the Revised edition of 1950 (17). Dykes's tunes must stand or fall as he wrote them. Romantic part-songs they may be, but they have a divine spark. His memorial is in every English-singing church.

Charles Steggall (1826–1905), a professor at the Royal Academy of Music, wrote some exhilarating hymn tunes. While his contemporaries were overworking the notes fah and te, he used them sparingly. The first five lines of St Edmund (A&M 53) are pentatonic; and in *Christchurch* (A&M 402) fah occurs only once and te twice in six lines. Steggall's tunes have a distinct character; it is a pity that more of them are not used.

Sir Joseph Barnby (1838–1896) and Sir John Stainer (1840–1901) did much to raise the standard of choral singing in this country, Barnby on the concert platform, Stainer at St Paul's Cathedral. Both were able musicians and composed a great deal. The years of their prime, however, coincided with the apogee of Victorian fashion for unctuous sentimentality in church music. As serious-minded musicians they provided music for the Church in the spirit of the age. In consequence, when reaction set in at the turn of the century, Barnby and Stainer, along with Dykes, were first into the pillory.

As an undergraduate I remember being introduced to Dr Sydney Watson, who shortly afterwards became organist of Christ Church, Oxford. He said, 'You are related to Sir

Joseph Barnby, aren't you?' I grinned somewhat apologetically and said, 'Yes—incredible fellow, wasn't he?' To which Dr Watson tactfully replied, 'He lived in an incredible age.' This should be remembered. The music of Barnby and Stainer is as true to its period as 'Rule, Britannia' to the eighteenth century. As to their hymn-tunes, literally dozens of hymn books were published between 1860 and 1890, and leading musicians were invariably asked to contribute. Barnby in his heyday received such a request nearly every week. Let us therefore judge these men not by their poorest work but by their best. Let Barnby be remembered for his bright, springing melody to 'When morning gilds the skies', his devotional tune to 'Jesu, my Lord, my God, my all' and his wedding hymn 'O perfect love'. A little sentiment is called for at weddings. His tune to the disused Easter hymn, 'O voice of the beloved' (A&M Old Standard 500) is worth reviving: it could be sung to 'O Father, all creating'. And let us be grateful to Stainer for his beautiful tune *In memoriam*, written for 'There's a friend for little children'; his much-loved settings of 'Author of life divine', 'Gracious Spirit, Holy Ghost', and 'Hail, gladdening light'; and, above all, the hymns in *The Crucifixion*, several of which have appeared in hymn-books with other words.

Sir Arthur Sullivan (1842–1900) was the most talented and versatile composer these islands had produced since Purcell. He was the son of an Irish military bandmaster and, like many great musicians, received his earliest training as a chorister. He wrote music of almost every kind, from song to symphony, but his gifts of sparkling melody and piquant orchestration are best displayed in the famous Savoy operas. His first composition was an anthem written at the age of 13. He maintained a lifelong interest in the Church. Much of his sacred music, sad to say, is substandard; but in some of his hymn-tunes there runs a golden thread that is unmistakably Sullivan. His Easter hymn, *Lux Eoi* (A&M 80), and his harvest hymn, Golden Sheaves (A&M 291), are deservedly popular. As for 'Onward, Christian soldiers', much criticism of this tune would be disarmed if its original time-signature were observed. In *The Hymnary*, for which it was composed, it was written in crotchets and marked for two beats in a bar.

Thus the monotony of repeated chords is relieved, and the tune assumes breadth and massiveness without losing its brightness and sense of urgency. The strong, martial rhythm should be maintained throughout, unimpeded by rallentandos and pauses between the verses. For congregational singing the most appropriate key is E flat.

Critics of the Victorian hymn-tunes blame the influence of Spohr and Gounod. Gounod was certainly admired by Barnby, who persuaded him to write nine tunes for *The Hymnary*. Spohr did not write hymns; but chromatic harmony, a characteristic of his style, was much emulated in this country. Chromaticism is effective on a big scale in the hands of a master, but when repeated, as in a hymn, it tends to cloy; moreover, it may have a debiliating effect on words. Dykes uses it well in 'Eternal Father', but four verses are enough. Now that the reaction against Victorian composers has run its course, we can appreciate without prejudice the value of their best work.

WE REACH THE TWENTIETH CENTURY. When one compares a tune by Gibbons with one of Croft's, and then with one of the minuet tunes of the eighteenth century, and then with Dykes, it becomes evident that roughly each century has its characteristic style. Moreover, since the revival of hymn-singing in England in the eighteenth century, a vast amount of disposable music has been written in the contemporary popular style, much of which served its purpose and passed out of use. Such were the fuguing tunes of the Methodist revival, and some of the songs sung by Sankey a century later. Can the same be said of the twentieth century? Has a style emerged that will characterise this age in years to come? Has this period also its share of disposable music?

Reaction on the part of musicians to the predominance of the Victorian hymn-tune began to show itself about the turn of the century. It was most marked in Anglican circles. Other denominations on the whole were slower to ditch old favourites. The music of the Presbyterian *Church Hymnal* 1898, however, showed characteristic care and discrimination; and in the same year *Catholic Hymns* included thirteen tunes by Richard Runciman Terry, who later became

Director of Music at Westminster Cathedral and in 1912 edited the music of *The Westminster Hymnal.*

I have already mentioned the *Yattendon Hymnal* (1899), in which Robert Bridges provided words to make fine old tunes available to Anglican congregations in their original form. Four significant Anglican hymn-books followed in the next decade: new editions of *Church Hymns* and *Hymns Ancient and Modern*, and two entirely new books—*The Oxford Hymn Book* and *The English Hymnal.*

Church Hymns, revised in 1903 under the musical supervision of C.H. Lloyd, though conservative, shows discrimination and taste. *The Oxford Hymn Book* (1908) was intended for college rather than church use. This gave its musical editor, Basil Harwood, who followed Lloyd as organist of Christ Church, Oxford, greater scope. Plainsong is well represented, Genevan psalms are given in their original from, chorales retain Bach's harmonies, and the best Victorian tunes are unaltered, including thirty-five by S.S. Wesley.

The unsuccessful revision of A&M in 1901 fell between two stools. Its chief fault was lack of variety. The compilers persisted in their policy of modifying tunes of earlier periods and so depriving them of their native strength. The number of Victorian tunes was reduced by half but, here again, some of those retained were reharmonised and so robbed of much of their essential character. Of new tunes the chief contributors were Stanford, Parry and Luard Selby (organist of Rochester Cathedral). It is surprising that Stanford and Parry, who did so much by example as well as precept to improve English music, did not on the whole succeed as hymn-composers. Stanford's tune Engelberg to 'For all the saints' is outstanding; but his eight other tunes, though of excellent quality, lack the common touch. Parry's twelve contributions, excepting Intercessor and his beautiful setting of Tennyson's 'Crossing the Bar' (which had already appeared in Church Hymns), are frankly dull. Parry's best tunes were not intended as hymns and not until later used as such: Repton ('Dear Lord and Father') was adapted from a ballad in his oratorio *Judith*; the fine tune to 'O praise ye the Lord' was the finale of his anthem 'Hear my words'; and then, in 1916, came 'Jerusalem'. Luard-Selby supplied 21 tunes. They are all well-written for choirs, but have not won the love of congregations, many being set to words either seldom sung or already wedded to a popular tune.

The 1889 A&M nevertheless continued in use until it was given a new lease of life in the Standard Edition of 1924.

The story of the *English Hymnal* (1906) and its aims has been outlined in chapter 1. Its young musical editor, Ralph Vaughan Williams, then unknown as a composer, came to his task with an open mind, uninhibited by prejudice or nostalgia. His study of folk-songs and Tudor music led him in a direction opposite to that of his predecessors. In EH plainsong is well represented; psalm-tunes and other old melodies are given in their original form, some to words from the *Yattendon Hymnal*; chorales have Bach's harmonies. Another feature of the book is the first appearance in England of French church melodies of the seventeenth century. Victorian tunes—many of them anyway excluded by copyright—are replaced by strong melodies with a popular appeal, notably folk songs, such as Monk's Gate, Forest Green, and Sussex, and Welsh tunes, like All through the night, Aberystwyth, Llanfair and S. Denio. EH has a few new tunes. Outstanding among them are those now inseparable from 'For all the saints' and 'Come down, O Love divine', by Vaughan Williams himself, and 'In the bleak midwinter' and 'From glory to glory' by his friend Holst.

The Public School Hymn Book (second edition, 1919) acknowledges its indebtedness to EH. It also contained four notable new tunes: Woodlands to 'Lift Up Your Hearts' by Walter Greatorex of Gresham's School, Holt, and three by William Harold Ferguson: Cuddlesdon, Ladywell and Wolvercote. These mainly unison melodies, clothed in rich, warm harmonies, are particularly effective when played by a school orchestra.

Songs of Praise (1925), an attempt to commend the best hymns to a wider public than EH catered for, was ideal for schools and did much to improve the literary and musical taste of the rising generation. Some credit for this is due to Martin Shaw (joint musical editor with Vaughan Williams); with his brother Geoffrey, an inspector of music in schools, he campaigned vigorously to raise the sights of school-teachers and clergy. The Enlarged Edition of 1931 has too many specially composed tunes, over fifty of them by the Shaw brothers. It is significant that most of those that have stood the test of time—notably Martin Shaw's Marching and Little Cornard and Holst's Thaxted (to 'I vow to thee, my country'), John Ireland's Love Unknown and Kenneth Finley's pentatonic tune Glenfinlas—are from the first edition.

The revision of the music of EH in 1933 shows the same trend. Most of the new tunes have failed to catch on. The greatest gain is the revision of the plainsong by J.H. Arnold.

Before we leave this period two names should be mentioned: first Sir Walford Davies, that genial Welshman whose broadcasts did much to spread musical appreciation in England and Wales—his musicianship and sensitivity to the rhythm of words is to be seen in *Hymns of the Kingdom* (1930) and his *Student's Hymnal* for Wales; and second G.R. Woodward, whose *Songs of Sion* is a treasury of European tunes (mostly of the seventeenth century) set to words that fit them rather than mutilated to fit English metres. It is a standard reference book: many of its items have been used as introits or short anthems.

Hymns Ancient & Modern Revised and *The BBC Hymn Book* were published within a few months of each other in 1950. As work on both had been begun before the Second World War, a comparison of their musical content is interesting. A&M is essentially Anglican and designed for use in church; the BBC book is interdenominational and intended for broadcasting. Both show the influence of EH. Plainsong, medieval church melodies, psalm-tunes, chorales, folk-tunes, Welsh melodies and British tunes of all periods have their place, with most of the old tunes given in their original form—a new departure for A&M. Indeed, it is significant that many hymns introduced to the churchgoing public by EH were by 1950 indispensable. It is in their attitudes to tunes of the nineteenth century that the books differ. The compilers of A&M, mindful of the rejection of their revision in 1904, were cautious in 1950: no really popular Victorian melody was left out; and, as far as copyright permitted, material from EH and SP was included. The BBC editors, however, seem to have considered that anything new must be better than what their grandparents liked. Many well-tried tunes were replaced by new ones, most of which, though well written, lack that indefinable something which touches the soul. It takes more than the second-rate new to supplant the second-rate familiar. Listeners to the Daily Service on BBC radio have frequently been irritated on hearing well-loved hymns sung to unfamiliar tunes. The most successful new tunes are those set to lesser-known words. Among these are two by Norman Cocker. Those who heard his astonishing organ-playing at Manchester Cathedral (and many cinemas) will remember his talent for bringing words to life. These tunes, set to different though carefully selected words in A&M 489 and 503, recall the old magic.

Both BBC and AMR include Cyril Taylor's Abbot's Leigh, one of the outstanding tunes of the century. I still prefer Austria for 'Glorious things of thee are spoken', but Abbot's Leigh suits other hymns as well. Of new tunes introduced by AMR the most distinguished are by Sir Sydney Nicholson, notably for 'We sing the praise of him who died' (215), 'Rise in the strength of God' (302), 'Hail the day that sees him rise' (610), and 'Lift high the cross' (633). Reviewing AMR 1950 for the *Manchester Guardian*, I wrote: 'Taken all round, this is the most comprehensive hymnal yet offered to the Church of England.' I still think it was.

Work on *The Cambridge Hymnal* began about 1957, though it was not published until ten years later. It was an attempt to provide morning assembly in schools with material at the same time more select and more varied than hitherto. Only about half of its 194 items are hymns in the traditional sense, and of these only fifty are familiar. The rest are religious lyrics by poets past and present (Auden and Eliot are represented), together with negro spirituals, carols, canons, rounds and descants. There are over fifty tunes by modern composers, including Bliss, Britten, Joubert, Mathias, Rubbra and even Stravinsky. The musical editor, Elizabeth Poston, contributed four tunes and many imaginative arrangements. In her preface she says: 'Hymn melody that is to be a communication needs to be essentially shareable.' How does a modern composer, freed from the shackles of the diatonic scale and text-book harmony, comply with this stipulation? Study *The Cambridge Hymnal* and see.

About the time when work on *The Cambridge Hymnal* began, another group came together with a quite different object. The Twentieth-Century Church Light Music Group was inaugurated by Geoffrey Beaumont, Patrick Appleford, Michael Brierly and others with a view to bridging the cultural gap between listeners to Radio 1 and Radio 3 (as those two networks came to be known.) The purpose is praiseworthy: Christianity is for all. Hymns, like sermons and scripture, should indeed be shareable (to use Elizabeth Poston's word). Furthermore, as we have already observed, there is no such thing as 'sacred music'. Any music sincerely used for a religious purpose becomes sacred. Previous generations have proved this from Bach to General Booth. In 1874 Verdi shocked many people by writing his Requiem Mass in his own idiom—the stage. Who would have expected to hear *Sanctus*, *Benedictus*, and *Hosanna* swept along in a tripping fugal dance lasting less than three minutes? Here we have a great genius dedicating his talents to God and so giving us a glimpse of the worship of heaven that is original, exciting and inspiring—as I hope heaven will be.

Beaumont and his friends would not claim to be Verdis, but they had his sincerity. They must at least be credited with introducing a new sound into worship, a sound which, as Malcolm Williamson (Master of the Queen's Music) has shown, can be expressed in a musicianly manner to the glory of God. Somebody asked Beaumont if he considered his tune to 'Now thank we all our God' an improvement on the chorale. His reply was characteristic: 'No, of course not. It all depends what it's for. If you want a formal vote of thanks, use the chorale; but if you simply want to say ta, use mine.' The Church Light Music Group had danced to this kind of music in the heydey of Fred Astaire and Ginger Rogers. In the Sixties, the age group their tunes appealed to were middle-aged parents. Their children were Beatle fans. Moreover, the group made the fatal mistake of setting their tunes to well-known words that had much-loved tunes of their own.

It was Sydney Carter's *Songs of Faith and Doubt*, written in his own less-holy-than-thou style, that captured the spirit of the Sixties. Apart from 'Lord of the Dance', set to an adapted shaker tune, the tunes of Carter's songs are his own. They are soundly constructed and not dated in style. They should have a reasonable life-span.

Since then, two new voices have sounded in hymnody. From the Iona Community, John Bell's tunes show partiality for the pentatonic scale and are, as to be expected, well written. The other voice comes from Graham Kendrick, son of a Baptist minister but himself an ecumenical Charismatic. Interviewed recently by Cole Moreton for the *Church Times*, he styled himself 'ordinary'. On the contrary, I should say he had exceptional talents. A self-taught guitarist, he has composed songs that have changed the lives of people all over the world. Sales of his record albums are phenomenal and could have made him rich; but he limits himself to 'a fairly average salary'. The rest is ploughed back into missionary enterprises and charities. When compared with Charles Wesley he replied, 'I don't think I could hold a candle to that man. I just want to feel I've served my generation.'

How does one start to criticise a man of such humility? I have already praised his lyrics for their strong scriptural content and timely message. His carelessness of rhyme and metre may be part of his appeal. But to treat music in the same way can rob the words of the power that music could give them. For example, even in his popular 'Shine, Jesus, shine', when singing the last line of the refrain—'Send forth your word, Lord, and let there be light'—I find myself wanting to raise my voice on the word 'word', not only because the tune needs a climax, but also because that word needs emphasis. The principles suggested in Chapters 7 and 8 for judging tunes are meant to be applied impartially to all hymns, even those written in a popular style. The more catchy the tune the more damage it will do if not matched to the words.

The twentieth-century hymn explosion shows no sign of abating. Although all the main-line hymnals have been revised recently, supplements are still appearing. Mention has already been made of *Worship Songs A&M* (1992) and the variety of material it offers. As a useful supplement to all existing hymnals it fulfills the promise of its preface. Musically it is a praiseworthy attempt to bridge the daunting cultural gap in today's society. The able and experienced musicians on the editorial team have shown that folk songs, ancient or modern, can be given a wider appeal by artistic treatment. This is a step in the right direction.

Has the twentieth century produced in this country a style of hymn-tune that will characterise it in years to come? My answer is yes. Its first half presents a worthy succession of composers whose overall style shows a preference for a strong, clean melodic line over dependence on harmonic effects. In the second half of the century two new sounds have emerged: the light-music genre, with oompah beat and adventurous rhythms, and a song-like type of hymn with introduction and interludes. As to the question of whether this century has produced its share of disposable music, it certainly has, and when all of it has been disposed of we may be proud of the gems that remain.

As we look back to the age of plainsong, it is possible to trace a clear line of descent to the modern hymn-tune, each age having left imperishable treasures which time has sifted out. With so rich and varied a heritage at our disposal, there can be no excuse for the perpetuation of the second-rate, or for the over-use on one hand, or the total exclusion on the other, of the music of any particular period or style.

PART THREE

HYMNS IN WORSHIP

10 THE ART OF CHOOSING HYMNS

REGULAR CHURCHGOERS, as well as clergy, must have noticed how greatly services can differ in effectiveness. There is that inspiring act of worship which gets off to a good start and seems to hit the right note from beginning to end; and there is another, in the same setting and conducted by the same person, which for no apparent reason falls flat. In both cases attendance has been good, reading and preaching clear, the music well sung. What can be lacking?

May not the answer lie in the choice of hymns? The hearty singing of well-chosen hymns gives corporate expression to our prayers and praises, clinches the message of readings and sermon, and implants them in the memory.

Some may deem this concern for effect misplaced. Worship, they will argue, is offered to God, who is spirit and does not need the aid of verse and music. That is true. It is also true, however, that only our best should be offered to God and what is inappropriate cannot be the best. Furthermore, we are bidden by St Paul to sing with understanding. The right hymns, like the right sermon, will help us. Choice of hymns, therefore, is an art worthy of careful consideration.

THE GENERAL PRINCIPLES are clear enough. First, Let hymns be selected well in advance. A monthly meeting of those responsible with the director of music is a worthwhile discipline. This will enable choir rehearsals to be planned. It is irritating for a choirmaster to be confronted with an unfamiliar tune at a rehearsal when, perhaps, the choir is under strength and other items press for attention. Similarly it is frustrating for the minister to be told that a desired hymn cannot be included because there is no time to rehearse it or find a suitable alternative tune. This mutual vexation can be avoided by advance planning. A new tune that has had a few minutes' practice for several weeks running will cause no panic at the last minute. Most congregations are prejudiced against the tune they don't know, but if the choir gives a confident lead much of this prejudice will be disarmed.

Next, a service should be a unity. Christianity has much to teach. A wise teacher will concentrate on one aspect at a time. People generally remember best what they have sung together. In an act of worship the prayers, readings and sermon may all have the same message; but if the hymns have been chosen haphazardly, or purely for popularity, they will certain distract attention from it and may well obliterate it altogether. If, on the other hand, prayers, readings, sermon and hymns reinforce the same theme, the congregation will go their way with its message ringing in their ears.

Unity of subject, however, should be balanced by variety in other respects. I would remind the reader of the four classes of hymns outlined in the first part of this book: hymns addressed to God about God, hymns addressed to God about ourselves, hymns addressed to us about God, and hymns addressed to us about ourselves. These correspond with the four sections into which an act of worship is generally divided: praise, prayer, teaching and exhortation. A judicious blending of these different approaches to the same subject will give a service variety without destroying its unity.

There should be variety of metre. A glance through the metrical index of a modern British or American hymnal will show that there is plenty of scope for contrast in the metrical shape of hymns. In A&M, for example, over 150 metres are listed, the verses varying in length from two to twelve lines. It should not, therefore, be necessary for a service to include an unbroken succession of four-liners.

There should be variety of period and style. Each period of church history has produced hymns to meet the needs of the day, often stressing a facet of the faith previously neglected. Most modern hymnals retain the finest hymns of all ages. Their inclusion in our services along with hymns of our own age will ensure not only variety of style but also balance in doctrine.

There should be variety in music. Here again we have a rich heritage. Plainsong and medieval melodies, German chorales, Genevan and Scottish and English psalm-tunes, and English hymn-tunes of the eighteenth, nineteenth and twentieth centuries are all available to enrich our worship. Each of these styles has its own charm and appropriate use. The austerity of plainsong is the more edifying when contrasted with, say, the elegance of Baroque; the severity of Puritan psalmody benefits from being offset by the warm humanity of the Romantic period; and so on. Worship in which all styles of music have their place is the most satisfying to the worshipper and the most complete offering of human gifts to their Giver.

There should be variety of key and time. A service in which all the music is in the same key or the same time—be it triple or common—is likely to be dull. Though many people may be unaware of the cause, the effect is still the same.

Variety is the basic principle of all programme-building, whether for a classical concert or a seaside show. Tastes differ, but too much of one thing palls. Variety has something for everybody. The same is true of public worship. Dullness amounts to irreverence. What wearies the worshipper is unfit to be offered to God.

Unity of subject and variety of approach and style, then, are things to aim at in choosing the hymns for a service.

In post-Reformation Britain the art of using hymns as a regular feature of public worship was initiated early in the eighteenth century by Dissenters, notably Isaac Watts. It was developed into a fine art by the Wesley brothers, whose hymn book of 1780 John Wesley described as 'a little body of experimental and practical divinity'. Thus to Congregationalists, and most of all to Methodists, their hymn book is their liturgy. Local preachers are trained in its use. Hymns are in their blood.

The Anglican Book of Common Prayer, with its cycle of collects and scripture readings, provided a superb system of teaching; but for reasons we have already discussed, it had no place for hymns, which did not become legal in the Church of England until well into the nineteenth century. Perhaps this is the reason why Anglican clergy have been trained to use the Prayer Book but not the hymn book. 'The Anglican, though he can write a hymn, cannot use it.' So wrote that shrewd and waggish Dissenter, Bernard Manning, in 1924. There are, of course, exceptions to this generalisation; but there is still, I find, enough truth in it today to justify my applying the foregoing principles to the services of the Church of England.

MORNING AND EVENING PRAYER, generally known as Matins and Evensong, being similar in structure, may as well be considered together. According to the Prayer Book they are daily offices. Hymns and sermon are authorised additions. The usual parish Sunday evening service, therefore, is in two parts: the Prayer Book office, and the sermon. Four hymns may be sung: the office hymn; a hymn in place of an anthem after the third collect; a hymn before the sermon; and a hymn after the sermon. The same applies to Matins.

The office hymn is so called because historically it belongs to the office and gives the service a seasonal note. It was dropped in the first English Prayer Book (1549) partly for want of suitable translations and partly because of Cranmer's reservations about hymns. Authority, however, was given for a hymn at Morning and Evening Prayer in the Injunctions of Queen Elizabeth (1559): 'In the beginning or at the end of common prayers either at morning or evening there may be sung an hymn or such-like song.'

The position of the office hymn varies a good deal in our churches. The singing of a hymn at the beginning of the service seems to have the authority of the Injunctions; but as the versicle 'O Lord, open thou our lips' makes no sense if a hymn has already been sung, one wonders if this was really intended. The custom of singing the office hymn before the *Magnificat* dates from the breviary. The structure of Evensong, however, differs from the structure of Vespers. In Evensong, the *Magnificat* is the proper link between the Old and New Testament lessons: this is blurred by the intrusion of a hymn.

The best place for the office hymn is before the Psalms. Following immediately after the response The 'Lord's name be praised' at Evensong, it is a fitting introduction to the unbroken recitation of scripture, alternately sung and spoken, which begins with the Psalms and ends with the *Nunc dimittis*. At Matins the office hymn will take its traditional place after the *Venite*, which must come first because it is a general invitation to worship. Before the Psalms the office hymn is well placed to introduce the Sunday theme on a note of praise.

The English Church of the Middle Ages appointed morning and evening office hymns for every season of the Church's calendar. A complete set is given in EH: we are indebted to the editors of both 1906 and 1986 for the fine translations they have provided. To follow all the ancient rules seems pedantic in these days. I doubt, for instance, whether there are many churches where 'Father, we praise thee' (NEH 149) is sung at Matins and 'O blest Creator of the light' (NEH 150) at Evensong every Sunday from June to the end of November.

A fairly short, objective hymn, bearing on the teaching of the day, will serve as an office hymn. So will an invitation to praise, such as 'All people that on earth do dwell' (A&M 100), 'Stand up and bless the Lord' (A&M 201), or 'Let all the world in every corner sing' (A&M 202). Many morning and evening hymns are also suitable. Some of these are genuine office hymns; 'Now that the daylight fills the sky' (NEH 151), or 'Before the ending of the day' (A&M 6). Others were almost certainly intended to serve as such, especially Bishop Ken's 'Awake, my soul' (A&M 1) and 'Glory to thee, my God, this night' (A&M 10).

Here a word may be interposed about two popular evening hymns, supposedly suitable only at the end of the service. A closer look at their text will show that this is not so. The subject of 'The day thou gavest, Lord, is ended' (A&M 16) (noted in chapter 3) is the world-wide Church. Its opening stanza says in effect, 'We have come together to end the day as we began it, praising God!' There is no reason, therefore, why it should not serve as an office hymn. And in 'At even, when the sun was set' (NEH 243), Henry Twells originally wrote 'At even, *ere* the sun was set' (A&M 9). The alteration was made later with the author's permission to bring it in line with Mark 1:32. Seven of the eight stanzas are in common use, but this hymn, addressed to Christ the healer, would be better balanced by the omission of verses 4 and 5 (of the seven). Thus shortened, it may be sung earlier in the service and so add significance to the final couplet:

Hear in this solemn evening hour,
And in thy mercy heal us all.

It is after the third collect that 'In quires and places where they sing, here followeth the anthem'. Before the state prayers were added at the Restoration of the monarchy, the office ended with the third collect, where the Injunctions of 1559 permitted 'a hymn or such-like song'. In Cathedrals and churches with choirs an anthem was sung. This may account for the rubric in the Prayer Book of 1662. The anthem, however, must be a worthy offering to God and an edifying experience for the congregation. Otherwise it is better to sing a hymn; in which case its position between collects and intercessions should be borne in mind. It should maintain the mood of devotion and not be noisy or long. Here is the ideal place for a hymn addressed to God about ourselves–a prayer-hymn related to the teaching of the day.

The hymns before and after the Sermon will ideally emphasise the preacher's them: the first preparing the mind, the second driving home the point. If the sermon be related, as is desirable, to the teaching of the service, hymns in line with the Sunday theme will be appropriate. Broadly speaking, a teaching hymn is suitable before the sermon and a hymn of exhortation or dedication after it. If the final hymn is to be a teaching hymn, the one before the sermon may be a prayer to the Holy Spirit—particularly Charles Wesley's 'Come, Holy Ghost, our hearts inspire', with its apt second stanza:

Come, Holy Ghost, for moved by thee
The prophets wrote and spoke.
Unlock the truth, thyself the key,
Unseal the secret book.

It is now happily available to Anglicans in AH 288, A&M 448, and NEH 348. Hymns about the Bible are appropriate, especially 'Help us, O Lord, to learn' (A&M 373); also prayers for inspiration, such as 'O thou who camest from above' (A&M 233) and 'Lord, be thy word my rule' (A&M 232).

The final hymn may be one of praise, prayer, teaching or

exhortation. In any case it should be the most stirring hymn of the service—and generally the longest, to allow for the collection. It should be robust, forward-looking and purposeful, setting the seal on all that has been said and sung.

Matins and Evensong are edifying services and I, for one, deplore their present decline. But the Church is right to restore the Lord's service to its place as the principal Sunday service for the faithful. The name Eucharist (meaning thanksgiving) is of early origin. Jesus, it will be remembered, 'gave thanks' at the institution of this service, which soon became the Church's supreme act of thanksgiving.

THE EUCHARIST is a service we are commanded to *do*, as distinct from Matins and Evensong, which are services of the word: read from the scriptures, preached from the pulpit, spoken to God in prayers, sung in psalms, canticles and hymns. Words are the essence of these services. The essence of the Eucharist is action: in particular, the actions of Christ at the Last Supper. He took bread and wine which his followers had brought; he blessed and broke; finally he gave them to the disciples. Hence the offertory, consecration and communion. Even the introductory service of the word includes two symbolic actions: the introit procession—the Church going to the Lord's Table to do as he commanded; and the Gospel procession—the Church going into all the world. Thus, whereas the hymns at Matins and Evensong illuminate words, those at the Eucharist give significance to actions. Ideally, therefore, each of the hymns at a sung Eucharist should coincide with the action it covers. If it is too short, it will necessitate padding by the organist, which, however good, will tend to distract attention; if the hymn outlasts the action, by, say, more than one verse, it can rob the action of significance and needlessly lengthen the service.

For the introit, custom varies. The choir may take its place and sing the introit—traditionally a psalm—while the priest and his attendants make their entrance. Generally, nowadays, priest, servers and choir proceed round the church singing a hymn. The symbolism of this I have already explained. Two observations may be added, First, it is better for the procession to form up in the church than in the vestry, so that the full choir can give the singing a strong start. Second, the Sarum order of procession—servers and priest before the choir—has the practical advantage of ensuring that, on arrival at a station or at the final object of the procession, the priest is in position to officiate.

The festivals have their own processional hymns. At other times the Sunday theme may point to an obvious choice. An objective hymn in praise of Christ is an apt introduction to the Lord's service and to most Christian subjects. Some such hymns are: 'Alleluia! Sing to Jesus' (A&M 262); 'At the name of Jesus', verses 1 to 5 (A&M 148); 'Come, ye faithful, raise the anthem', omitting verses 3 and 6 (A&M 145); 'Christ is the King' (A&M 345); 'Hail to the Lord's anointed', omitting verses 4 and 5 (A&M 142); 'When morning gilds the skies' (A&M 146); and 'Ye servants of God, your master proclaim' (A&M 149). Or an invitation to worship may be sung: 'All people that on earth do well' (A&M 100); 'Lo, God is here! let us adore' (NEH 209); 'O worship the Lord in the beauty of holiness' (A&M 49); or 'Stand up and bless the Lord' (A&M 201).

The Gradual too is a procession, though a short one. The hymn, therefore, should be short. It links the Epistle, or Old Testament reading, with the Gospel; accordingly it should be related to one or other of these passages or to the collect. A short, general hymn on scripture is sometimes appropriate, especially: 'Can man, by searching, find out God?' (A&M 438); 'Come, Holy Ghost, our hearts inspire' (A&M 448); 'Help us, O Lord, to learn' (A&M 373); 'Lord, be thy word my rule' (A&M 232); 'Lord Jesus, once you spoke to men' (A&M 392); 'Praise we now the word of grace' (A&M 417); or 'The prophets spoke in days of old' (A&M 513).

For the offertory, a fairly long hymn is needed. The significance of this action has been set forth by several writers, notably Bishop Henry de Candole in his little book, *The Church's Offering* (Mowbray 1935, revised 1951). Bread and wine—food and drink—representing ourselves, our souls and bodies, are brought to the altar by members of the congregation. Usually the collection is taken and offered with the oblations, since it is our wealth, as well as our life and work, that is offered. The next action is that of Christ, the true celebrant at every Eucharist. He takes our offering (our life) and consecrates it, joining it with his own 'full, perfect and sufficient sacrifice'. He then gives it back to us at the communion rail, full of his presence and power. Thus, through him, our lives are regularly renewed and made fit to be offered to God in love and service.

Three excellent modern hymns are based on this teaching: 'Christians, lift your hearts and voices' (A&M 447), by Canon J.E. Bowers, a former Vicar of Ashby-de-la-Zouche; 'Dear Lord, to you again our gifts we bring' (A&M 352), by Tom Gaunt, a former Precentor of Winchester Cathedral; and 'O holy Father, God most dear' (A&M 410), by Monsignor Tomlinson. The last, too short for the offertory, may be sung during the communion. The tune Sussex Carol certainly fits the words, but is so closely associated with Christmas that I prefer to keep it as a carol. Wesley's Colchester (A&M 243) carries these words well, as does Barnby's St Chrysostom (AMR 202). Also suited to the offertory are hymns on worship, such as: 'Angel voices ever singing' (A&M 163); 'Lift up your hearts' (A&M 241); 'Lord, enthroned in heavenly splendour' (A&M 263); and 'O praise ye the Lord' (A&M 203). Besides those there are hymns of self-dedication, like 'O Jesus I have promised' (A&M 235). Any hymn of suitable length related to the Sunday theme is appropriate here.

HYMNS FOR THE COMMUNION ITSELF address the question of what we receive at the communion rail. The answer of the Prayer book catechism is: 'The body and blood of Christ, which are verily and indeed taken and received by the faithful in the Lord's Supper'. That this statement (part of the section added to the catechism at the request of Puritans at the Hampton Court conference in 1604) is basic Christian belief is attested by the variety of communion hymns in most hymn books. What still tends to divide us is how this mystery of grace is conveyed. We come closest to unity in our hymns. Therefore I here invite my readers to step aside from the main purpose of this chapter and study carefully the communion hymns in the two most comprehensive Anglican hymnals, A&M and EH.

We begin with three hymns by St Thomas Aquinas, written at the request of Pope Urban IV in 1264 for the then new festival of Corpus Christii. The translations differ in wording, but their meaning is as near to the Latin as English verse in the same metre can get. The first is *Pange, lingua, gloriosi corporis mysterium* (A&M 252, NEH 268). Note the scholarly precision and reserve with which the author defines the doctrine of the Eucharist. His use of the metre and opening words of the sixth-century passion hymn (A&M 59, NEH 78) is no doubt a deliberate linking of the 'memorial' with the 'sacrifice once offered' which it shows forth (1 Corinthians 11:26). Even in verse 4 he declares that faith alone can discern the mystery of Christ's presence in the sacrament. From this *Tantum ergo* (verses 5 and 6) follows logically.

The second is *Verbum supernum prodiens* (A&M 253, NEH 269), more concise and more explicit, leading to the prayer, *O salutaris* (verses 5 and 6). And the third is *Lauda, Sion, Salvatorem* (AMR 622, NEH 269), a sequence in twelve stanzas, seldom sung in full by Anglicans, though parts of it make good communion hymns. In verse 5 the memorial aspect of the sacrament is blended with the sacrificial; in verse 9 St Paul's warning against taking it unworthily (i.e. without repentance) is stressed (1 Corinthians 11:26). *Panis angelorum* (verse 11) refers to Psalm 78:25: 'So men did eat angels' food.' See also the second line of *O esca viatorum* (AMR 389, NEH 300), and compare Josiah Conder's 'Bread of heaven, on thee we feed' (A&M 271, NEH 276) and Chatterton Dix's 'Alleluia, sing to Jesus', verse 3 (A&M 262, NEH 271).

Adoro te (A&M 254 NEH 308), also attributed to St Thomas Aquinas, stresses the real presence of Christ in the 'blest memorial of our dying Lord'. Other notable hymns of Latin origin are *Ave verum corpus* (A&M 268, NEH 289)—immortalised by the musical settings of Byrd and Mozart—and John Mason Neale's 'Draw nigh and take the body of the Lord' (AMR 386, NEH 281), based on a seventh-century text.

There are also two Greek hymns which create the right frame of mind in which to make communion: 'Let all mortal flesh keep silence' (A&M 256, NEH 295), translated from the fifth-century Liturgy of St James by Gerard Moultree; and 'Here, while the cherubim within the veil' (AMR 391), translated by C.S. Phillips from the sixth-century Cherubic Hymn.

From Germany we have 'Deck thyself, my soul, with gladness' (A&M 257, NEH 280), by the seventeenth-century burgomaster Johann Franck. This hymn, made available to us in Catherine Winkworth's lovely translation, dwells on the element of joy in the Eucharist. G.R. Woodward's 'Dearest Jesu, we are here' (A&M 269) is based on another seventeenth-century German hymn.

Among Anglican writers William Bright, Regius Professor of Ecclesiastical History at Oxford at the end of the nineteenth century, has given us that summary of eucharistic teaching, 'Once, only once' (A&M 261, NEH 304) which we studied in chapter 5; and its companion prayer, 'And now, O Father, mindful of the love' (A&M 260, NEH 273), in which 'our dearest and our best' are brought before Christ to be offered to the Father in his 'one true, pure, immortal sacrifice'. Likewise all those we remember in the intercessions are brought into the context of offertory, consecration and communion in William Jervois' beautiful hymn, 'Wherefore, O Father, we thy humble servants' (A&M 275, NEH 313).

Vincent Coles contributed two hymns: 'Almighty Father, Lord most high' (A&M 267), intended as an offertory hymn, but too short for use as such; and 'We pray thee, heavenly Father'. It is interesting to compare his two versions of the latter: the first (A&M 264) written before his ordination, the second (NEH 311) when he was Principal of Pusey House, Oxford.

Bishop Heber's little gems, 'Bread of the world in mercy broken' (A&M 270, NEH 277) and 'O most merciful' (AMR 410, NEH 301), need no introduction.

Percy Dearmer, always ahead of his time, wrote two hymns that threw new light on the Eucharist. The first (NEH 90), written in about 1906, begins thus:

Holy God, we show forth here
Jesu's death our sins to clear,
Jesu's life our life to be,
Jesus's love the world to free.

It is more than the death of Jesus that we 'show forth'. Were not his humble birth and life of love sacrificial acts? (Philippians 2: 6–8). Dearmer's other communion hymn, 'As the disciples, when thy Son had left them' (A&M 341), written in 1930 and based on the *Didache*, to place the Eucharist in its historic setting, has influenced much recent thinking on this service.

The view that Christ is the true celebrant at every Eucharist is supported by Canon G.W. Briggs, who in 1931 wrote 'Come, risen Lord, and deign to be our guest' (A&M 349, NEH 279), based on the Emmaus supper—Luke 24: 18–31. It is implied in other communion hymns, particularly 'For the bread which you have broken' (A&M 456), by the American hymnologist Louis F. Benson, who died in 1930.

Free-Church hymn-writers are well represented. Besides Conder's 'Bread of heaven', Philip Doddridge, another Dissenter, has given us 'My God, and is thy table spread?' (A&M 259, EH 320). The second stanza begins:

Hail, sacred feast which Jesus makes,
Rich banquet of his flesh and blood!

Note too the use of the word 'victim', in the third stanza, in an age when even Anglicans considered it popish.

Now read Charles Wesley's 'Victim divine' (NEH 309), written at about the same time, which proclaims the real presence of Christ in the sacrament. In another communion hymn, 'O thou eternal victim, slain', though much altered (A&M 395), Wesley addresses Christ as both priest and victim:

Thyself the lamb for ever slain,
Thy priesthood doth unchanged remain.

We find this form of address based on Hebrews 9:11–12, echoed a century later by the Anglican, Chatterton Dix, in the last verse of 'Alleluia, sing to Jesus' (A&M 262, NEH 271).

For what the Lord's service means to the average worshipper it would be hard to find simpler expression than in the hymn by Horatius Bonar, founder member of the Free Church of Scotland: 'Here, O my Lord, I see thee face to face'. Of his original ten stanzas, written in 1855, AH (376) gives six, EH (312) four, and A&M (274) three.

Present-day writers of all denominations are concerned with the relevance of the Eucharist to daily life. I have mentioned the Tomlinson hymn 'O Holy Father, God most dear' (A&M 410). From Bell and Maule of the Iona Community come 'Before we take the body of our Lord' (WS 8); 'Bread is blessed and broken' (WS 11), in which communion is seen as memorial, means of grace, pledge of forgiveness and meeting with Christ; and Song of the supper (WS 86), an account of the Last Supper in modern terms, set by Alan Wicks to a charming Scottish folk-song. The Methodist Fred Pratt Green, in 'An upper room' (A&M 434), highlights our Lord's washing of his disciples' feet (John 13: 1–17): 'For service, too, is sacrament.' To Fred Kaan it is the 'sacrament of care—(A&M 403 verse 3). Brian Wren, of the URC, in 'I come with joy to meet my Lord' (A&M 473), sees at the Lord's table 'Man's true community of love in Christ's communion bread'. 'Living Lord' (A&M 391, NEH 297)—words and music written in about 1960 by the Anglican, Patrick Appleford—is a sincere expression of praise, prayer and self-commitment to Christ in the pop style. Sung slowly, in the tempo of a blues rather than a foxtrot, and with expression—an awestruck hush at the words 'Son of God'—it can be deeply moving.

Over a century ago Colonel Turton wrote the prayer for unity:

> O thou, who at thy Eucharist didst pray
> That all thy Church might be for ever one (A&M 265, NEH 302).

The Church has sung it devoutly ever since. Today we are nearer the answer to that prayer.

Other devotional hymns are appropriate here, especially: 'Jesu, thou joy of loving hearts' (A&M 255, NEH 292); 'Jesus, these eyes have never seen' (A&M 245, NEH 389);

'Jesu, grant me this I pray' (A&M 136, NEH 382); 'Just as I am, without one plea' (A&M 246, NEH 294); 'O thou who camest from above' (A&M 233, NEH 431); 'Of all the Spirit's gifts to me' (A&M 503); 'There in God's garden' (A&M 514); and 'Christ be with me' (NEH 278). On a recent visit to my first parish, St Aidan's, Rochdale, I was impressed by the singing during communion of the Taizé song 'Eat this bread'.

IF, AS RECOMMENDED in the new rite, the *Gloria in excelsis* is restored to its traditional place before the service of the word, the post-communion hymn is the one hymn specifically authorised by scripture: 'And when they had sung a hymn, they went out ...' (Mark 14:26). With this hymn on their lips, the family of God disperses with the nature and power of Christ within them.

The final hymn, then, should reflect the joy, conviviality and fellowship that befits those who have just been guests at Christ's table. Examples are: 'Filled with the Spirit's power (A&M 359); 'Give me joy in my heart' (A&M 459); 'Happy are they, they that love God' (A&M 176, NEH 369); 'In Christ there is no east or west' (A&M 376, NEH 480); and 'Sent forth by God's blessing' (A&M 510).

Thanksgiving for blessings received is expressed in: 'Fill thou my life' (A&M 200), omitting verses 5 and 7); 'From glory to glory' (A&M 276, NEH 286); 'King of glory, King of peace' (A&M 194, NEH 391); 'The King of love my shepherd is' (A&M 126, NEH 457); 'Through all the changing scenes of life' (A&M 209, NEH 467); and 'When all thy mercies, O my God' (A&M 109, NEH 472).

The hope of Christ's continued presence shines from: 'Guide me, O thou Great Redeemer' (A&M 214, NEY 368); 'Love divine, all loves excelling' (A&M 131, NEH 408); and ' 'Tis good, Lord, to be here' (A&M 318, NEH 178).

Faith in the Church is voiced in: 'City of God' (A&M 173, NEH 346); 'The Church of God a kingdom is' (A&M 169, NEH 483); and 'Thy kingdom come! on bended knee' (A&M 178, NEH 500).

Dedication and service are urged in: 'Fight the good fight' (A&M 220, NEH 359); 'Forth in thy name, O Lord, I go'

(A&M 239, NEH 235); 'Oft in danger, oft in woe' (A&M 210, NEH 434); 'Rise up, O men of God' (A&M 418); 'Strengthen for service' (A&M 421, NEH 306); 'Take my life' (A&M 249); 'Teach me, my God and King' (A&M 240, NEH 456); and 'When I needed a neighbour' (A&M 433).

And the call to witness is heard in: 'O God of truth (A&M 222)'; 'Tell out, my soul' (A&M 422, NEH 186); and 'We have a gospel to proclaim' (A&M 431, NEH 486).

The post-communion hymn should, of course, relate to the teaching of the day. One of those hymns should be chosen with that in mind. They are hymns that I myself have used to suit one or another of the Sunday themes in non-festal seasons. Between Advent and Trinity Sunday a seasonal hymn is usually appropriate. As the last hymn is likely to linger longest in the memory, its aim should be to send people out with something to remember.

11 FEASTS, FASTS AND OTHER OCCASIONS

THE HYMNS FOR CREATION, Christmas, Epiphany, Easter, Ascensiontide, Pentecost and Trinity need no introduction here. Most of them have been discussed in part 1. It is important to remember, though, that to the vast majority of worshippers these hymns give each passing season its special character. The omission of an old favourite at, say, Christmas or Easter can cause not only sadness but also loss of valuable teaching. It is wise, therefore, to keep seasonal hymns for their own season. To sing even their tunes at other times blunts their impact. There is still scope for the use of good new material, but let it supplement, not replace, the old.

Hymns proper to the fasts are also in danger of neglect. The Advent hymns are loved by many Anglicans; there is a thrill of expectancy about them. 'Hark, a thrilling voice is sounding', 'Creator of the starry height' and 'Lo, he comes' have special relevance to the first Sunday in Advent. 'Sleepers, wake' (or 'Wake, O wake') is suitable on any of the first three Sundays. At least one hymn on the Bible and 'Thou whose almighty word' should be added on the second Sunday; 'On Jordan's bank' and an Ember hymn on the third Sunday, as well as 'Hills of the North, rejoice' (What a pity the line 'Hark to the advent voice' has gone). On the fourth Sunday (according to the 1980 sequence) 'Hark the glad sound', 'O come, O come, Emmanuel' and hymns on the Blessed Virgin Mary are appropriate. Particularly suited to the second or fourth Sunday is 'Long ago, prophets knew', written by Pratt Green for the old carol tune *Pesonent hodie*. Holst's fine arrangement of OBC and H&P has a two-bar introduction which has the double advantage of establishing the relentless rhythm and the Dorian scale, both of which are strong features of the tune. Of course all Advent hymns may be used on any Sunday in the Season.

Then there is *Lent*: 'A somewhat unattractive time Which hardly lends itself to rhyme'.

So John Betjeman affectionately heralds its approach in his poem 'Septuagesima'. Lent need not be unattractive where hymns are concerned. There are two without which to many worshippers the season would not be complete. One is 'Forty days and forty nights'. The original version by G.H. Smyttan appeared in the *Penny Post* for March 1856. There were nine stanzas of four lines. The shortened and altered version in A&M 56 and NEH 67 was made by Francis Pott in 1861. The version given in AH 141 is from the *Hymnal Companion* and nearer to the original. The other is 'Christian, doest thou see them' (A&M 55, NEH 65, AH 137). John Mason Neale, England's greatest translator of ancient hymns, was the first to adapt Greek hymnody for use in the Church of England. This hymn appears in his *Hymns of the Eastern Church* as 'Stichera for the second week of the Great Fast', attributed to St Andrew, a notable hymn-writer who became Archbishop of Crete in 692. But nothing even remotely like it has been found in Greek hymnody; it is therefore assumed to be Neale's own creation. This Archbishop came for a short while under the influence of the Monothelite heresy, but recanted and returned to the orthodox faith. Neale, who was steeped in the thought and literature of these Greek Christian writers, may well have picked up—perhaps from one of St Andrew's homilies—the idea of warning others not to listen to clever persuaders. 'Troops of Midian' refers to Numbers 25, which tells of the attempts of these crafty neighbours to corrupt and so weaken Israel. Such persuaders still afflict the Church. Also appropriate to Lent is 'Forgive our sins as we forgive', by Rosamund Herklots.

Passiontide hymns are fully covered in chapter 5.

Rogation days, strictly speaking, are the three days before Ascension Day, associated from ancient times with prayers for God's blessing on the crops. By 1928 the previous Sunday, though not a fast, was 'commonly called Rogation Sunday' and devoted to prayer. The ASB collect and Gospel (for Year 2) refer to this subject, though the given theme is 'going to the Father'. In these troubled times, when the problems of Church and state seem beyond the wit of man, I should like to see Rogation Sunday kept as a day of national prayer, with the restoration of Walsham How's 'To thee, our God, we fly' and Montgomery's hymns 'prayer is the soul's sincere desire' and 'Lord, teach us how to pray aright'.

Graham Kendrick's 'If my people who bear my name' also strikes the right note.

The Naming of Jesus is kept on 1 January: what better name to start the year with? Any hymn on the holy name is suitable. Bishop Dudley Smith's 'O Christ, the same through all our story's pages' commends the past, the present, and the future to Christ, thus combining the two thoughts of the day. And Christmas hymns are still in season.

The presentation of Christ in the Temple is also called Candlemas on account of the beautiful ancient ceremony to symbolise Simeon's prophecy that Jesus would be 'a light to lighten the gentiles'. The office hymn 'See how the age-long promise of a Saviour' (NEH 156) covers the subject well. Ellerton, in 'Hail to the Lord who comes' (A&M 314, NEH 157, AH 441), tells the Gospel story and relates it to the prophesy in Malachi 3. Hymns on the Blessed Virgin Mary are appropriate, particularly Heber's 'Virgin-born, we bow before thee'; also hymns in praise of Christ, especially *Phōs Hilaron* (A&M 8, NEH 247, AH 54), 'Love divine' (A&M 131, NEH 408, AH 625), and 'Angels from the realms of glory' (A&M 39, AH 93: verses 2 and 3 may be omitted on this occasion). Suitable carols may also be sung.

The Transfiguration seems to be far too important to be overshadowed by Mothering Sunday, when families gather to pay tribute to their mother and expect timely guidance on family life or perhaps on Mother Church. Now that the Epiphany season, when the Church dwells on the manifestations of Christ's godhead, continues virtually from 6 January until Lent, would it not be better to commemorate the Transfiguration, his final glorification, on the Sunday before Lent, rather than the theme 'Friend of sinners', which belongs more to Lent itself? Of hymns on the Transfiguration, ' 'Tis good, Lord, to be here', by John Armitage Robinson, and 'Not always on the mount' (A&M 561), by the American Unitarian, Frederick L. Hosmer, make the point that moments of vision are granted to us, as to the chosen apostles, to give a deeper and richer meaning to the cares of daily life. Brian Wren's 'Christ upon the mountain peak' bids us join Moses, Elijah and the three disciples in adoration of their glorified Master. Other relevant hymns are: 'Blest are the pure in heart'; 'Christ, whose glory fills the skies'; 'Jesus, these eyes have never seen; and 'Teach me, my God and King'.

AMONG THE SAINTS, the Blessed Virgin Mary, as sole human agent chosen to co-operate with God in the redemption of the world, rightly has pride of place. It is significant that the Book of Common Prayer of 1662 assigned five days in the year to her honour.

Of the ancient office hymns for these occasions, the most commonly used today is that translated 'The Lord (or God) whom earth and sea and sky' (A&M 309, NEH 181): it is now believed to be the work of Venantius Fortunatus. It is an exposition of Gabriel's greeting in Luke 1:28. Later hymn-writers have further developed this theme. 'Her virgin eyes saw God incarnate born' (A&M 310, NEH 182), a fine cento from a longer poem by the seventeenth-century Bishop Ken, was made for EH in 1906. Early in the nineteenth century Reginal Heber, before he became a bishop, wrote 'Virgin-born, we bow before thee', a hymn addressed to Christ in praise of his mother. It is remarkable for its poetic beauty, scriptural teaching, unity of thought and economy of words. Sir Henry Baker's Shall we not love thee, Mother dear?' (AMR 515, NEH 184) is trite but true. We do well to remember that in honouring Mary we follow the example of her Son.

Three hymns by recent authors have added something fresh. In 'For Mary, Mother of our Lord' (A&M 360, NEH 161), J. R. Peacy describes her as 'brave': Cyril Taylor in his commentary draws attention to this 'unique address of the Virgin'. The editors of the NEH have deprived the hymn of this distinction by omitting the verse in which it occurs. To accept the challenge of Gabriel's message meant risking the misunderstanding of her fiancé and friends, giving up the prospect of a normal family life and taking on the responsibility of rearing a unique child, who early in life would himself be misunderstood and executed. Mary's ready reply, 'Be it unto me according to thy word', was indeed a brave act of faith. George Timms's hymn, 'Sing we of the blessed Mother' (NEH 185), is a useful processional, based on the joys and sorrows of Mary; and Bishop Dudley-Smith's 'Tell out, my soul' (A&M 422, NEH 186), though not *about* Mary, is a singable modern version of her *Magnificat*.

While there is no shortage of good hymns on saints in general, remarkably few on individual saints have come off. St Andrew does have the classic 'Jesus calls us'. But the Christmas saints tend to get lost in the rush: their feast should be honoured even when they fall on a Sunday. For St Stephen, Heber's 'The Son of God goes forth to war' is the best available hymn. On this occasion the verses on the apostles may be omitted. It is a pity Jan Struther's 'When Stephen, full of power and grace' (SP 219) does not appear in recent hymnals. For St John the Evangelist, Keble's 'Word supreme before creation' is perhaps too abstruse for a hymn. One of the hymns for evangelists, however, may be used; so may 'Of the Father's heart begotten', which echoes the prologue to the fourth Gospel. For Innocents' Day there is Laurence Housman's 'When Christ was born in Bethlehem' (NEH 203), originally written for children. As these hymns are related to Christ's incarnation, they may be sung alongside Christmas hymns, so introducing a healthy variety to the teaching of the season.

For St Paul, John Ellerton's 'We sing the glorious conquest' (A&M 313, NEH 155) holds its place; and 'Paul, the preacher, Paul the poet' (AMR 542), written by Amy Sayle in 1937, describes the saint in vivid, economical phrases which all can understand. Most missionary hymns are also appropriate.

St Joseph is a welcome newcomer to the Anglican calendar. His name first appeared in the Roman calendar in the fifteenth century; but as the date, 19 March, seems to have no significance, Anglicans might find it more helpful—as in the East—to commemorate him during Christmastide, when his story is fresh in the mind, rather than in Lent. As for hymns, 'Lord, hear the praises of thy faithful people' (NEH 160) is a serviceable record of St Joseph as 'guardian of the Christ child', spouse and protector of Mary, and an example to us all. A new hymn, however, dwelling on his self-effacing humility, considerateness, devotion to his craft and, above all, faith in God's guidance, would be timely.

For St Philip and St James we have Percy Dearmer's refreshing hymn 'The winter's sleep was long and deep' (EH 221), set to a delightful May Day carol. Which James are we celebrating? James the Less, of whom nothing is known, or the author of the Epistle? ASB assumes the former, BCP and Dearmer the latter. The important thing is what they can teach us. As a practical parish priest I have found the latter more helpful. 'Thou art the way' (A&M 128, AH 455) is also relevant to St Philip.

St Matthias (now 14 May) is adequately dealt with by the scholarly dean, Henry Alford, in 'The highest and the holiest place' (AMR 545, NEH 165). As for St Barnabas in AMR 550 too much has been made of the mistranslation 'son of consolation' (Acts 4: 36), and not enough of that good saint's generosity in placing his property at the disposal of the Church, in welcoming St Paul after his conversion and in giving John Mark a second chance.

For St John the Baptist the Venerable Bede in the early eighth century wrote *Precursor altus luminis* (AMR 553, NEH 169); and later in the same century Paul the Deacon, a monk of Monte Cassino, was inspired by the same subject to write the fine hymn *Ut queant laxis* in thirteen sapphic stanzas: five are translated in NEH 168 and three in A&M 315. We also have Dearmer's 'Lo, in the wilderness a voice (A&M 384, NEH 170). The hymns 'Soldiers, who are Christ's below' (A&M 302, NEH 450) and 'Stand up, stand up for Jesus' are in line with the character of the Baptist; as is the Advent hymn, 'On Jordan's bank', with his message.

For St Peter, 'O Rock of ages, one foundation' (AMR 554) was written by H.A. Martin for *Church Hymns* in 1871. It is addressed to Christ and full of scriptural allusions: in verse 1 to Matthew 16:18 and Isaiah 60:18; in verse 2 to Matthew 16:16; in verse 3 to Matthew 14:26–31; in verse 4 to Luke 22:61; and in verse 5 to John 21:16. Mrs Alexander's hymn, 'Forsaken once and thrice denied' dwells on Peter's denial, as if the cock on almost every steeple were not a sufficient reminder. Verse 3, however, brings home the fact of Peter's repentance, and verse 4 points the question:

How oft his cowardice of heart
We have without his love sincere,
The sin without the sorrow's smart
The shame without the tear!

Bishop Walsham How, in 'Thou art the Christ' (A&M 317, NEH 172), dwells on Peter's confession. He mentions the denial and, in verse 4, commends the patience, faith, courage and love which the saint achieved in the power of the risen Christ. Among hymns common to saints, 'Disposer supreme' stands out as particularly appropriate to Petertide; and these general hymns are also relevant: 'Just as I am, without one plea'; 'King of glory, King of peace'; 'Christ is our corner-stone'; 'The Church of God a kingdom is'; and 'City of God, how broad and far'.

Moreover, the recent association of ordination with this season brings in the Ember hymns.

St Thomas's day is now transferred from 21 December to 3 July, as in the Syrian Church. In the early Greek Church the first Sunday after Easter was known as St Thomas's Sunday. For the practical purpose of teaching the faith this would seem more suitable to the saint's commemoration. The Easter hymn 'Ye sons and daughters' (A&M 74, NEH 125) is appropriate. A striking new hymn on the patron saint of doubters is 'Who dreads, yet undismayed' (A&M 534), written by J.R. Darbyshire—later Archbishop of Cape Town—for *Songs of Praise* in 1930.

St Mary Magdalene is represented by the medieval hymn *Collaudemus Magdalenae*. An earlier version beginning *Pange lingua Magdalenae* has been attributed to the thirteenth-century writer Philippe de Grêve. An English translation by Laurence Housman is given in EH 230 and 231, and a digest in three verses by C.S. Phillips in AMR 556.

St James the son of Zebedee is remembered for his mother's request that he and his brother might have seats of honour in Christ's kingdom, and the Lord's reply (see NEH 175). But Mrs Alexander, in 'For all thy saints, a noble throng' (AMR 557), cites occasions when James was one of the privileged three to be present with the Master, and his execution by Herod.

The collect and lessons for St Bartholomew's day refer only to the general apostolic mission; hymn-writers have cast about for something to say. C.S. Phillips (AMR 562) and Jan Struther (SP 236) have written hymns drawing the moral that it is not only famous deeds that win the crown of glory. Athelstan Riley (NEH 179) has cleverly contrived an acrostic on the apostles in general, the initial letters of its sixteen lines spelling SAINT BARTHOLOMEW. Only John Ellerton has pursued the suggestion, for which there is strong internal evidence, that the Bartholomew of the first three Gospels may be the Nathaniel of the fourth. His hymn 'King of saints, to whom the number' (written for *Church Hymns 1871* and last printed in A&M as 419 in the Old Standard Edition of 1924) is addressed to Christ; it refers in verse 3 to John 1:45–50 and 21:1–14.

The feast of St Simon and St Jude on 28 October has to make do with the general hymns on the apostles, though 'Christ is our corner stone' accords with the collect. In any case it is overshadowed by the brilliant festival of All Saints.

THE EVANGELISTS form a subgroup among the saints. Isaac Watts's 'How beauteous are their feet' (A&M 301) we analysed in chapter 1. 'Spirit of Jesus', by C. S. Phillips (AMR 511), is a thanksgiving to the Holy Spirit for the four Gospel-writers, drawing the distinction between the first three, who based their message on the evidence of eye-witnesses, and the fourth, who reflects the ripened faith of the Church in the next generation.

St Mark's day is 25 April. Mrs Alexander's 'From out the cloud of amber light' (AMR 548) is based on Ezekiel 1, but its symbolism is too nebulous for present-day worshippers. More to the point is Laurence Housman's 'The saint who first found grace to pen' (NEH 163), based on the opinion of scholars that St Mark's was the first Gospel to be written.

St Matthew, now celebrated on 21 September, is still represented by William Bright's hymn, 'He sat to watch o'er customs paid' (AMR 563, NEH 189, AH 450): it dwells on the call of the tax-collector, and leaves the authorship of the Gospel an open question.

St Luke's day is kept on 18 October. Considering that we

owe a quarter of the New Testament—his Gospel and Acts—to the 'beloved physician', but for whose friendship and medical care St Paul might have died of overwork, it is remarkable that Luke has not had better coverage in hymns. Archbishop Maclagan's 'What thanks and praise to thee we owe' (AH 448) was dropped by AMR in 1950 in favour of H.D. Rawnsley's 'Saviour, who didst healing give' (AMR 567, NEH 194). My favourite hymn on St Luke was written some years ago by Gilbert Hudson, at my request, for the dedication of a church to him. As a sample of its style, I quote the second verse:

> We praise thee for the angel tongues,
> Their rural symphony divine,
> And all the holy scenes and songs
> That in those pages ring and shine,
> By the beloved physician penned,
> Afflicted Paul's enduring friend.

Slightly adapted for churches of which Luke is not patron saint, and sung to the unison tune written for it by my father, a pupil of Stanford, this hymn would make a fine processional.

St John the Evangelist (27 December) has already been discussed under Christmas saints.

THE ANGELS, too have their hymns. 'Stars of the morning' (A&M 319, NEH 193) is a free rendering of lines from a ninth-century Greek Canon for the 'bodyless ones'. The scriptural basis is Job 38:7: 'When the morning stars sang together and all the sons of God shouted for joy'. This is poetry: the writer may mean the stars themselves, personified as in Psalm 148, or angels, the 'sons of God' in the answering phrase. The latter is certainly the meaning of the hymn, which in the same stanza tells of their singing the *Trisagion* 'thrice holy': a reference to Isaiah 6:3. In stanza 2 they are described as nearest to God in heaven and guardians of humans on earth. In stanza 3, thrones, principalities, virtues and powers are the supposed ranks of angels referred to in Colossians 1:16, Stanza 4 is omitted in A&M. Here Neale cites three archangels with names derived from their Hebrew meanings: Michael, God's champion, in Daniel 10:13 and Revelation 12; Gabriel, enlightener, in Daniel 8 and Luke 2; and Raphael, who appears only in the Apocrypha as healer of Tobit and companion of Tobias. The climax of the hymn is the stanza beginning 'Then, when the earth was poised in mid-space'. This calls for unison. The word 'shouted', in the last line, is the only word I allow my choir to shout; they never forget. The final stanza is a prayer to God for his angels' protection.

'Christ, the fair glory of the holy angels' (A&M 321, NEH 190), a ninth-century Latin hymn, translated in the same sapphic metre, is a prayer through Christ for the help of the archangels named by Neale above. 'All praise be to God' (AMR 566), by the poet Bridges, was written for children. Note the monosyllables. This simple account of the ministry of angels needs no explanation and satisfies all age-groups. The stately eighteenth-century tune, Spetisbury, carries these words perfectly.

It is surprising that, in days when so much is made of the duty of service, it has never been linked with the services of angels. The Michaelmas collect is addressed to 'God who ordained and constituted the services of angels and men in a wonderful order'. I take this to imply that as angels are appointed by God to be our spiritual guardians, so in God's plan our role is to give each other material help. A Michaelmas hymn on these lines would fill a gap. Surely this beautiful festival is worth a Sunday observance—say the last in September, to keep the first in October for harvest.

HARVEST THANKSGIVING still attracts many worshippers who are not regular churchgoers. The Church should strengthen such links as a means of evangelism. As Rogation Sunday might be regarded as a day of prayer, so might harvest festival be a day of general thanksgiving for all God's blessings on human effort, of which the crops are a colourful token. If this were fixed as the first Sunday in October, the annual cycle could begin the following Sunday, allowing the three essential Sunday themes, creation, fall and faith, to take place before All Saints and Remembrance. To rename the day Harvest and General Thanksgiving and to decorate the church accordingly would ensure its continued popularity.

The traditional harvest hymns have much to teach: 'on God's goodness, 'Let us with a gladsome mind'; on man's co-operation with God, 'We plough the fields'; on the harvest of souls, 'Come, ye thankful people, come'; and on the eucharistic offering of ourselves, 'To Thee, O Lord, our hearts we raise'. The same point is made by Andrew Young in his poem, 'Lord, by whose breath all souls and seeds are living' (A&M 486).

John Arlott's fame as a cricket commentator rested on the fact that, being a poet, he could paint a picture in words. 'God, whose farm is all creation' (A&M 370) is one of three hymns he wrote for *The BBC Hymn Book* (1951). It is a simple prayer for God's blessing on 'our calendar of care'. Fred Kaan, in the bold amphibrachic lines of 'Now join we to praise the Creator' (A&M 500), reminds us of our duty to share God's blessings. Fred Pratt Green wrote the estimable hymn 'For the fruits of his creation' (A&M 457) to match Francis Jackson's equally estimable tune, East Acklam. These newcomers, each in his own way, give wider application to the season. Their hymns are useful supplements to the old stock.

FOR A DEDICATION FESTIVAL, the date will depend on local history. It is an occasion to thank God for his Church, the body of Christ, empowered by the Holy Spirit, militant on earth, triumphant in heaven. We praise Christ for giving us the sacraments of baptism and holy communion, whereby we receive and maintain relationship through him with God. The Church is our link with eternity. All hymns on the Church give this timely teaching. (See chapters 3, 5 and 6.) So does 'Lo, God is here!' (AMR 249, NEH 209)—With, in these days, 'wondrous' preferable to 'dreadful' in line 2.

Two Latin hymns deserve special notice. One is *Urbs beata* (A&M 332, NEH 204), conveniently divided into two parts. 'Blessed city, heavenly Salem', is about the Church in heaven, whose 'living stones' were fashioned in this world with 'many a blow and biting sculpture' for their place in glory. 'Christ is made the sure foundation' turns to the Church on earth: two stanzas based on Ephesians 2:19–22 are followed by two of prayer for those who gather in the building, in the manner of Solomon's prayer in 1 Kings 8:28–33. The other is *Christe cunctorum dominator alme* (NEH 210). The translation—'Only begotten, Word of God eternal'—by Max Blacker is in the sapphic metre of the original. It contains much scriptural teaching about the Church and its sacraments expressed in clear terms. The only unusual word is 'laver' (font) in verse 4.

THE SACRAMENT OF BAPTISM should be administered publicly at a service with a regular congregation. Good reasons are given in the Prayer Book rubric on public baptism. However, in these days many of those who bring their children to Anglican clergy to be baptised do not normally attend church. Indeed, they have little or no knowledge of the meaning of baptism. While on the one hand this is a depressing thought, on the other there is hope. It shows that beneath the parched surface of apparent indifference there are still some living roots of residual faith which watering could revive. Such nourishment the vicar will try to give on visiting the parents beforehand. Another hopeful sign is the number of relatives and friends who come with them to the service. An attempt to give instruction during such a service is liable to be drowned by the crying of the baby or the uncontrolled capers of other children, welcome though they are. Where talking fails, however, singing may succeed. A good hymn of fundamental teaching may get the message across.

Since Dean Alford's classic, 'In token that thou shalt not fear', has disappeared from our latest hymnals, what is left? A&M has four hymns suitable for a baptism. They are: 'Eternal God, we consecrate' (452), by Robert Dobbie, a prayer for the child's welfare with a passing reference to the duty of sponsors in verse 2 and 'means of grace' in verse 4; 'God the Father, name we treasure' (466), by Basil Bridge, which prays to God the Father for care, to the Son for grace, and to the Holy Spirit for power; 'We praise you, Lord, for Jesus Christ' (521), a thanksgiving for the benefits of baptism, appropriate after the rite; and 'Christ, when for us you were baptised' (442). Here Bland Tucker reminds us that Jesus Christ followed up his own baptism with a life of service, and asks for grace to do the same.

The Editors of NEH have rewritten R.S. Hawker's 'Sing to the Lord the children's hymn' and added two verses on baptism. HTC provides ten hymns under the heading Christian Initiation. Most are prayers or praise, but four are addressed to us about baptism. Three are by Michael Saward: 'Baptised in water' (based on Romans 6:3–4), 'Have you not heard?' and 'My trust I place in God's good grace'; and one by Michael Perry, 'Now through the grace of God we claim'. All contain teaching, but not enough. What I should like to see is a hymn in clear, singable verse, spelling out the scriptural answers to questions I have often been asked: 'Why is baptism necessary? What are the outward signs? What are the blessings conferred? Perhaps there should be another stating the duties of the baptised; or in the case of infants, the duties of parents and godparents.

A CONFIRMATION is one of the occasions for hymn-singing where fresh thought would be particularly welcome. There is no objection to the well-tried favourites: 'Soldiers of Christ, arise', 'Come, Holy Ghost', 'My God, accept my heart this day', and 'O Jesus, I have promised'. But they are overworked.

At confirmation the candidates ratify the promises made in their name at baptism, when they became learner members of Christ's Church. Hitherto their sponsors have been answerable for them. Now they throw away their L-plates and take the wheel themselves. But they are not alone. A hymn about the Church will remind them of this: 'Glorious things of thee are spoken', 'The Church of God a kingdom is', or 'Firmly I believe and truly'. Before confirmation, they will need a prayer to the Holy Spirit: 'O thou who camest from above', 'Come down, O love divine', 'Eternal Ruler of the ceaseless round', 'Breathe on me, breath of God', or 'Holy Spirit, come confirm us' (A&M 471, NEH 140). And after confirmation, dedication is in point: 'Take my life',

'God be in my head', 'I bind unto myself today', or just the verse 'Christ be with me'.

A new hymn on the importance of regular communion would fill a gap.

A BRIDE AND BRIDEGROOM will often appreciate guidance in their choice of hymns for their wedding. 'Praise, my soul', The King of love', 'Lead us, heavenly Father', and 'O, perfect love' are fine hymns, well fitted to the occasion, but they are getting a little threadbare. Occasionally there are requests for lyrics that are not hymns at all. Also it is frequently forgotten that 'the twenty-third Psalm to Crimond' properly belongs to funerals rather than weddings. Sometimes a tune sung and enjoyed at school will be asked for without regard to the suitability of the words. Requests for 'Turn back, O man', or 'Come, O thou traveller unknown', though rare, are not unheard of. The popular hymn 'Dear Lord and Father of mankind' certainly voices lofty aspirations; yet, in the context of a wedding, its first and last verses are apt to suggest thoughts far from the mind of the author and embarrassing to the bride and groom.

Some couples give a lot of thought to their wedding hymns, as these few examples show: 'Come down, O Love divine'; 'Come, gracious Spirit, heavenly dove'; 'Father, hear the prayer we offer'; 'Happy, are they, they that love God'; 'Lord of all hopefulness'; 'Praise to the Lord, the almighty'; 'Teach me, my God and King'; 'The King of love, my shepherd is'; 'Through all the changing scenes of life'; 'Fill thou my life'; 'Father, Lord of all creation'; and 'Give me joy in my heart'.

A hymn of praise may be sung for the bridal procession. I am sure Richard Wagner would agree that this is preferable to a watered-down version of his bridal march from *Lohengrin* out of context.

At the great festivals, certain seasonal hymns are suitable at a wedding. At Christmastide, for example, 'O little town of Bethlehem' is appropriate.

AT FUNERALS, it is not always easy to persuade mourners to think of resurrection rather than death. Here are some hymns that strike the right note:

'Let saints on earth in concert sing', 'He wants not friends that hath thy love', 'Light's abode, celestial Salem', and 'There is a land of pure delight'. There are also Easter hymns, like 'Jesus lives!' Such hymns as these give the assurance of the Christian gospel at a time when it is most needed and most appreciated. It is a pity that 'On the resurrection morning' has gone out of use. It has been a comfort to many mourners. One of my parishioners, who had been a devout communicant from his teens to the last week of his life, died at the age of 95. His funeral took place on the feast of the Epiphany. The hymn chosen was 'As with gladness, men of old'. Never have I heard the last two verses sung with such feeling.

12 PROBLEMS AND POSSIBILITIES

WHERE HYMNS ARE CONCERNED, two problems confront the Church today: the problem of taste and the problem of teaching.

The problem of Taste is an old one. In 1925 I.A. Richards, a prominent literary critic of his day, wrote in *Principles of Literary Criticism*: 'With the increase of population the problems presented by the gulf between what is preferred by the majority and what is accepted by the most qualified opinion has become infinitely more serious and appears likely to become threatening in the near future.' Though he was referring to literature, his statement applies to other fine arts, especially music.

Tastes, like talents, naturally differ. It would be a dull world if they did not. Both are largely hereditary; but taste at least can be broadened. Apart from native preferences, the taste of a particular generation will depend on the influences to which young people are exposed in their formative years. The ideal of education is not to create uniformity of taste but to broaden it and so widen the field of enjoyment. With this aim, in the years just before and after the Second World War, the study and appreciation of the fine arts was encouraged in schools. Poetry and music in particular were taken seriously. Radio, and later television, played a part in familiarising all age-groups with the works of the great masters.

The early post-war years I spent in Manchester, where I regularly attended the Hallé Concerts. I remember noticing the high proportion of young people present. Indeed, though there were two performances of the same programme each week, you had to book early to get a seat. As for church music, mention must be made of the Royal School of Church Music, founded in 1927 and given its present title in 1945. Sydney Nicholson, organist of Westminster Abbey, a talented musician with vision and a flair for organisation, gave up his post at the Abbey to become the founder and director of the School of English Church Music, as he called it. This is now the RSCM, a world-wide fellowship of devoted choristers who aim at the highest standards of singing to the glory of

God. Again, the Education Act of 1944 provided for daily assembly in state schools, with prayers and hymns, and for the teaching of scripture. Thus by the mid-Fifties school-leavers knew at least what Christianity stood for, and were familiar with the best hymns sung in the main Christian churches.

Then came the Sixties, followed by the crisis in authority which we discussed in chapter 1. This reversed the hopeful trends of the previous decades, with the result that today, a generation later, the problems facing the Churches have worsened. Public taste, far from being broadened, is now polarised. Opportunities to study the fine arts at school still exist; but the motive is no longer self-improvement so much as money. Musical children study music not in order to enjoy it as a hobby but to become professionals. Choral singing, a mainly amateur activity, is neglected. This has posed a twofold problem for the churches: a shortage both of competent amateur organists and of recruits for the choir.

The present problem of religious teaching likewise has its roots in the Sixties. For most of the past thirty years the 1944 Act has been barely observed. (In fairness it should be added that in 1944 nobody had envisaged the comprehensive school, where it is often impossible to accommodate some 2000 children for assembly in a single hall.) Religious teaching in our multi-faith society is largely left to parents.

If I seem to be overstating the adverse effects of the crisis in authority, perhaps a personal reminiscence may help. One of my earliest childhood memories is of going to church with my parents on Advent Sunday, having learnt the collect for the day. My mother had explained the collect and added that we would be singing the hymn 'Hark, a thrilling voice is sounding', in which words from the collect would come again. As we sang the line 'Cast away the works of darkness', we glanced at each other and smiled. That was the beginning of my life-long interest in hymns. How many parents today would know either the collect or the hymn or, if they did, could be sure of hearing them in church?

Another problem is that the welfare state—a truly Christian concept—has raised the question whether the church is relevant to modern society. St Paul was on an easier wicket at Athens where he noticed an altar with the inscription 'To an unknown god'. There he had a starting-point. The Athenians were at least looking for a god. Where does one start in a society that feels no need for God?

Canon W.H. Vanstone, relates in his book entitled *Love's Endeavour, Love's Expense* his experience when visiting the housing estate, still without a church, of which he was to be the first vicar. 'Without exception people were courteous: without exception they were indifferent.' They were fulfilled and contented in the pleasant homes and surroundings provided by the council. He goes on to tell that this depressing experience led him to see the Church not so much as a service to the community but rather as the community's response to God's love. This became the basis of his long and fruitful ministry in that parish. Canon Vanstone's insight is a good starting-point for today's Church as it faces the same problem.

Towards the bridging of the gulf in taste some helpful steps have already been taken. The dedicated staff of the RSCM, having campaigned for some forty years for the highest standards, must have been taken aback by these adverse trends. To their credit, however, they came to terms with them and sought, through their wide membership, courses and summer schools, to help clergy, worship committees and choristers to discriminate between good and bad songs in the pop style. In 1972 the BBC published *Come and Sing* for children. This modest collection of 72 hymns contains over twenty well-known traditional ones side by side with colourful new lyrics in terms that appeal to the modern child, set for the most part, to strong, singable tunes in the new folk style. This book is widely used and due, I think, for a new edition. In 1992 appeared *Worship Songs Ancient & Modern*. Its able team of editors declare in their preface: 'It was the apparent need for songs of a style that bridged the present gap between the classic hymns and the popular chorus . . . that caused the publishers of Hymns A&M to offer this collection of 100 worship songs to the Church.' In my opinion this is the most important step towards closing the taste gap yet taken.

Taizé songs are in a class by themselves and certainly

deserve mention here. However, although I have been much moved by a Taizé service, I have come to the conclusion that it is the service as a whole—the intimacy of a small room, candlelight, readings, prayers, silences and chants, as much as the songs—that creates the atmosphere of reverence. Sung in isolation, except perhaps at communion, the songs have not the same appeal.

An encouraging sign today is the rich variety of hymns and songs offered in the BBC television programme *Songs of Praise*. Regrettably, few churches have the resource to present them so lavishly. It is surprising, though, what can be done on a smaller scale. Robert Peers joined my choir at Bramhall Parish Church at the age of seven and continued, boy and male alto, until he left school. After taking his degree he married Anne, a Bramhall girl, and got a teaching post in Tyneside. The church they joined had no choir, the vicar being a congregational-participation fan. Robert, however, soon formed a small group of singers who met at his house. Eventually he persuaded the vicar to let them sing an occasional anthem in church (unrobed). He drew mainly on the Bramhall repertoire—Tallis to Joubert. Later they were joined by instrumentalists. Largely to please the vicar, they began to include modern songs. The Cramlington St Nicholas Music Group is now twenty years old. They still continue their varied diet, so enriching tastes on both sides. In his intriguing account of the group, Robert writes, 'Just as part of the sacrifice of musical leadership is to sing things one wouldn't choose, surely the sacrifice of being a member of a church is to love those whom God has put us with.'

So we come back to the problem of evangelism and the need for Christian education. This remains the primary duty of the Church; but the Church can only teach those who come to it, and a society which considers the Church irrelevant is not likely to come. Much, therefore, will depend on the schools. The National Curriculum now provides for basic religious instruction at primary level. Two difficulties, however, remain. One is denominational. Religious instruction would be a lot easier if the Churches spoke with one voice. The other is that suitable teachers are hard to find. Few of those educated in the last thirty years have either the knowledge or the conviction. Indeed, it is not fair to expect it of them.

To each of these problems hymns could be the key. It is Christ's will that his Church should be one. It is therefore our duty to work and pray for unity. Great strides have been made in this century. Much prejudice has been overcome. The denominations are now on speaking terms and co-operate at many levels. Moreover, it is realised that unity does not necessarily mean uniformity. Our forms of worship are a matter of taste. These may be carried on in a unified Church while we grow closer together in belief. On the whole the things that divide us are not what we believe but what we refuse to believe. Personally I would rather appear before my Judge having believed too much about him than too little. It is not likely that unity will be achieved by top-level conferences alone. It must start in the pews and in the aisles with the realisation that each denomination has contributed precious gifts we all need. Not least among these are our hymns.

Next to the Bible, nothing unites Christians more than hymn-singing. When hymns are sung, denominational difficulties roll away. Indeed, all modern hymnals are more ecumenical than is generally realised. We noted in chapter 1 the diverse denominations represented in the present hymn explosion, and in chapter 10 the rich variety of traditions enshrined in our communion hymns. It may interest the reader to know that of the 533 hymns in A&M (1983), 306 are also in the Methodist *Psalms and Hymns* (1983), 278 in the URC *Rejoice and Sing* (1991), 183 in *Baptist Hymns and Worship* (1991), and 143 in the RC *Complete Celebration Hymnal* (1984). *The Song Book of the Salvation Army* (1986) contains over 200 classics commonly used by most Churches; but as they also sing a great many modern hymns with the aid of a projector, a precise figure cannot be given.

Now consider twelve of the best-known hymns in the English singing world: Watts's—'O God our help in ages past' and 'When I survey the wondrous cross'; Wesley's—'Jesu, lover of my soul' and 'Hark! The herald angels sing'; Bunyan's—'Who would true valour see'; Bonar's—'I heard the voice of Jesus say'; Duffield's—'Stand up, stand up for

Jesus'; Whittier's—'Dear Lord and Father of mankind'; Samuel Johnson's—'City of God'; Newman's—'Praise to the holiest'; Heber's—'Holy, holy, holy'; and Lyte's—'Praise, my soul, the King of heaven'. It is worth reflecting that Watts was a Congregationalist, Charles Wesley a founder of Methodism, Bunyan a Baptist, Duffield a Presbyterian, Bonar a Scottish Free Churchman, Whittier a Quaker, Samuel Johnson a Unitarian, Newman (when he wrote those lines) a Roman Catholic, and Heber and Lyte Anglicans. When we think how great our sense of loss would be if we were deprived of any of these, we begin to see how much we owe to each other; and that is a step nearer the unity for which Christ prayed.

As to the problem of teachers: need we worry? A good hymn, as I have tried to show, is a complete act of worship in itself, and often lingers in the memory longer than the spoken word. Even nowadays most children prefer singing to listening to an address. Regular school assembly—in groups if necessary—consisting of nothing more than the singing of a good hymn could leave a life-long impression. Perhaps even Tennyson would agree that, like prayer, more things are wrought by hymns than this world dreams of.

GLOSSARY

amphibrach: a short–long–short metrical foot
anapaest: a short–short–long metrical foot
antiphonal: where one side of a choir answers the other
Augustan age: in English literature the early eighteenth century
binary: of a melody, having two sections
caesura: a pause in rhythm or sense in the middle of a line of verse
cento: selected lines or verses from a longer poem
common metre (CM): with syllables per line in the pattern 8 6 8 6
conjunct: of a melody, with motion by steps
dactyl: a long–short–short metrical foot
Didache: an early Christian document on church teaching and practice
disjunct: of a melody, with motion by leaps
double common, long or short metre (DCM, DLM, DSM): with the stated pattern repeated in eight-line verses
fuguing tunes: Hymn tunes, popular in the eighteenth century, in which certain syllables are sung to a florid outburst of notes, others repeated, as in the choral fugues of that age.
faburden: harmonisation of a tune with the melody in the tenor
gathering note: a two-pulse note at the beginning of a line
grace note: extra ornamental note in an eighteenth-century tune
Gregorian tone: plainsong chant for psalms, etc. The opening phrase is generally called the intonation
iamb: a short–long metrical foot
inversion: of a melody, turning it upside down so that rising passages fall and vice versa. (A chord is said to be inverted when its lowest note is not the root. Thus in the chord *doh me soh*, the lowest note is *doh*, which is also the root. Its first inversion is *me soh doh*^{1}, the lowest note being *me*; the second inversion is *soh doh me*^{1}, the lowest being *soh*.)
interval: difference in pitch between one note and another

long metre (LM): with syllables per quatrain in the pattern 8 8 8 8

Metaphysical: A term applied to certain seventeenth-century poets, e.g. Donne and Herbert, given to paradoxical comparisons

modal: written in the scale of one of the Greek modes

melisma: florid outburst of notes on one syllable

monothelite: The heresy that Christ has one will and one nature

neum: a group of notes in plainsong

office: a statutory church service other than the Eucharist: e.g. Matins, Evensong

passing note: A note or notes passing from one chord to another, as in Bach's chorales

pentameter: a line of five feet

pentatonic: scale of five notes: *doh ray me soh la*

quatrain: a verse of four lines

rallentando: slowing down

ritenuto: holding back

root: fundamental bass of a chord, not necessarily the actual bass

sapphic: giving a quatrain of three trochaic pentameters followed by one shorter line

short metre (SM): with syllables per quatrain in the pattern 6 6 8 6

stanza: verse

suspension: the holding of one or more notes of a chord until after the next chord has sounded

ternary: form of melody in three sections, A B A

tessitura: the general lie of the notes of a melody (or part)—high or low

trochee: a long–short metrical foot hence trochaic

trope: a sung embellishment of the text of the mass or office before the 12th century

FOR FURTHER READING

Julian: *A Dictionary of Hymnology* (Murray 1907)

Percy Dearmer: *Songs of Praise Discussed* (OUP 1933)

Bernard Manning: *The Hymns of Wesley & Watts* (Epworth 1942, 1988)

Henry Betts: *The Hymns of Methodism* (Epworth 1945)

Miller Patrick: *Four Centuries of Scottish Psalmody* (OUP 1949)

Erik Routley: *Hymns & Human Life* (Murray 1952)

Maurice Frost: *English & Scottish Psalm & Hymn Tunes* (SPCK & OUP 1953)

Erik Routley *Hymns & The Faith* (Murray 1955)

W.K. Lowther Clarke: *A Hundred years of Hymns A&M* (Clowes 1960)

Maurice Frost: *Historical Companion to Hymns A&M* (Clowes 1962)

Hugh Martin (ed.) *Baptist Church Hymn Book Companion* (Psalms & Hymns Trust 1962)

John Barkley: *Handbook to the Church Hymnary* (OUP 1979)

Frank Colquhoun: *Hymns that Live* (Hodder & Stoughton 1980)

David Perry: *Hymns & Tunes Indexed* (Hymn Society & RSCM 1980)

Erik Routley: *Christian Hymns Observed* (Mowbray 1984)

Cyril Taylor: *Hymns for Today Discussed* (Canterbury Press Norwich 1984)

Lionel Dakers: *Choosing & Using Hymns* (Mowbray 1984)

Tyler Whittle: *Solid Joys & Lasting Treasure* (Ross Anderson 1985)

Ian Bradley: *The Penguin Book of Hymns* (Penguin 1990)
Charles Robertson (ed) *Singing the Faith* (Canterbury Press Norwich 1990)
Baker & Welsby: *Hymns & Hymn Singing* (Canterbury Press Norwich 1993)
Brian Castle: *Sing a New Song to the Lord* (Darton Longman & Todd 1994)

INDEX OF HYMNS
(First lines)

GENERAL INDEX